BORN TO LIE

FROM
THE BIRTH CERTIFICATE
TO HEALTH CARE

Dr. David L. Goetsch
Dr. Archie P. Jones

WHITE HALL
PRESS
FREEDOM IN PRINT

Born to Lie

From the Birth Certificate to Health Care

© 2009 by David L. Goetsch and Dr. Archie P. Jones

Published by **White Hall Press**
44 Mountain Park Drive
White Hall, WV 26554

Printed in the United States of America.

Cover design by Joseph Darnell

ISBN13: 978-1-61623-309-9

Also by the Authors

Liberal Tyranny in Higher Education:
How You Can Fight Back

CONTENTS

INTRODUCTION

Arrogance and Deceit
in the Oval Office

This book is about a man of ironic and disturbing contradictions: Barack Obama. On one hand, he is the first African-American ever elected President of the United States, but on the other hand he may not even be eligible to serve in that office. As a presidential candidate, Barack Obama promised the American people an administration that would be open and transparent, but as President he has shown himself to be capable of both arrogance and deceit. As a presidential candidate, Barack Obama promised to be a president of the people, but as President he has shown himself to be capable of blatant imperiousness.

As a presidential candidate, Barack Obama promised to help bridge the racial divide in America, but as President he has shown a disturbing propensity for the practice of racialism. As a presidential candidate, Barack Obama promised to be a post-partisan leader, but as President he has used his Congressional majority to steamroll the opposition party and the millions of Americans it represents. As a presidential candidate, Barack Obama did his best impression of George H. W. Bush's no-new-taxes promise for middle-class Americans, but as President he is already using key staff members as surrogates in waffling on the promise.

This book is first and foremost about the paramount question concerning Barack Obama's eligibility to serve as President of the United States: Is he a natural-born American citizen? But it is also about other critical issues of transparency and trust. It is about promises made during the presidential campaign and quickly broken after the election. It is about arrogance, imperiousness, deceit, cover-ups, and obfuscation in the Oval Office. In addition, it is about mean-spirited attacks by President Obama's most faithful supporters—aided and abetted by the press and media—on Americans who exercise their Constitutional rights of dissent and have the temerity to question this president.

Questions That Should Be Asked and Answered

We developed this book around five questions we think should be asked by Americans about President Obama. We believe that these are five questions the press and media would ask and expect satisfactory answers to if the President were not their chosen son. We also believe that these are questions that should be asked in the interest of the integrity of the political process, journalistic ethics, and the rule of law. One chapter is devoted to each of the following questions:

- What is the birth certificate issue all about?

- Is there room for reason in debates about the birth certificate and transparency?

- Why do so many Americans find it difficult to trust President Obama?

- Why does President Obama lack credibility with so many Americans?

- Putting aside the birth-certificate issue, is President Obama really an American at heart?

Chapter One explains the birth-certificate issue, what is at stake concerning it, why answering the questions surrounding the President's citizenship is important, why the founders insisted that presidents be natural-born citizens of the United States, and why allowing Obama and his supporters to brush off the birth-certificate issue by labeling all doubters as conspiracy-theorists, sore losers, or racists is disingenuous and unacceptable.

Chapter Two deals with the practice of President Obama's supporters lumping all doubters and questioners together and labeling them as wackos. This chapter makes the case that although there are, no doubt, people whose questions about the President's citizenship are based on less than commendable motives, there are also many patriotic Americans whose questions are the result of genuine concern for the integrity of the Constitution and the future of our country. These Americans should be taken seriously and treated with respect. Chapter Two makes the case that *ad hominem* name calling by Obama's supporters is not a worthy response when serious issues of Constitutional integrity and transparency in the Oval Office are raised.

Chapter Three answers the question about why so many Americans do not trust President Obama. This chapter deals not with President Obama's citizenship but with how he has chosen to handle questions about it. It also examines a series of promises made by Obama, the candidate, which were broken by Obama, the President. This chapter asserts a theme that runs throughout the book—that we do not believe the Congress or courts have either the inclination or political will to remove President Obama from office even if it is found to be certain that he is not a natural-born American citizen. Therefore, President Obama will have to answer to only one tribunal: the court of public opinion. This is why it is so important that questions about his citizenship and promise of transparency be asked.

Chapter Four explains why President Obama lacks credibility with so many Americans. The principal issue dealt with in this chapter is religion. President Obama denied that America is a Christian nation and even called the United States one of the largest Muslim nations in the world. He is wrong on both counts, a fact that has undermined his credibility with a substantial number of Americans—particularly Christians.

Chapter Five speaks to what may be the most pertinent question about President Obama: Is he an American at heart? We do not believe the American people will ever see definitive proof that the President is an American citizen. For reasons of his own, President Obama has chosen to lock up any and all records that might shed light on this Constitutional question. However, Americans will learn by Obama's actions whether he is an American at heart, regardless of whether he is one in fact. This chapter explains how President Obama's propensity for socialistic government programs makes many Americans doubt his commitment to the America established by our founding fathers.

Acknowledgment of WorldNetDaily

We are pleased to acknowledge the leadership WorldNetDaily has provided in investigating and reporting on the issue of President Obama's birth certificate and recommend their excellent DVD, *A QUESTION OF ELIGIBILITY: Is Obama's presidency constitutionally legitimate?* produced by Joseph Farah. This DVD can be purchased from Patriot Depot at http://www.PatriotDepot.com/

Full Disclosure by the Authors

The authors wish readers to know from the outset that we did not support Barack Obama's candidacy to be President of the United States. In the interest of full disclosure, we also wish to make clear that we fall into the demographic cohort consisting of white Southern male conservatives over the age of forty (well over). Having said these things, we also wish to make clear that we did not oppose President Obama because of his race. In fact, we both respect the historical significance of his election. Like many Americans we welcome what having our country's first African-American president represents, but we would have preferred that the individual who won that distinction be Condolezza Rice or Thomas Sowell.

We wrote this book not because of our philosophical opposition to President Obama, but because we are concerned about the Constitutional issue of his citizenship, broken promises of transparency, his naiveté in foreign policy, a glaring lack of experience, his unshakable belief in a socialist response to America's economic woes, and a surprising propensity for arrogance and deceit. We are not conspiracy theorists, do not get our news from the tabloids, and fully understand that Elvis is dead. We are not sore losers or racists. We, like many others who share our concerns, are Americans who believe in the rule of law, the supremacy of God, and the vision of the founders. These are the reasons why we wrote this book.

ONE

What is the Birth Certificate Issue All About?

"Truth can never win unless it is promulgated. Truth does not carry within itself an antitoxin to false-hood. The cause of truth must be championed, and it must be championed dynamically."

—William F. Buckley, Jr.
God and Man at Yale, 1951

What if the first African-American president turned out to be African but not American? This simple question contains the seeds of one of the most controversial issues ever to surface concerning an American president. Barack Hussein Obama made history by becoming the first African-American ever elected to the presidency of the United States. Consequently, the validity of his citizenship is an issue with ramifications that go well beyond the Constitutional crisis the controversy could precipitate.

To many people, Obama's election was a transformational event that they responded to on a deeply emotional level. For these Americans, the election was more than a political victory, it was vindication. For example, an African-American friend of one of the authors claimed that he voted for Obama even though he disagrees vociferously with his politics. Consequently, to question Barack Obama's citizenship is to threaten not just the results of a historic election, but the sense of long-awaited vindication felt by many of Obama's supporters. This fact goes a long way toward explaining why so few Americans seem to be able to discuss the issue of President Obama's citizenship objectively and reasonably.

Congress declared Barack Obama president-elect of the United States on January 8, 2009. He took the oath of office and began his tenure as president on January 20th. At this point much of the world celebrated the unprecedented election of America's first African-American president. Even his detractors recognized his election as a historic event. However, temporarily lost in all of the celebratory commotion was a simple but critical question that had been circulating for some time: *Is Barack Obama an American citizen?*

Some claimed that in electing Obama, America had chosen not just its first African-American president, but its first non-American president. For years an unresolved controversy about his citizenship has swirled around Barack Obama. His election to our nation's highest office has only fanned the flames of this controversy. His own unwillingness to clear up the controversy has just added fuel to the flames.

The question of his citizenship would seem easy enough to answer. Just do what every other American has to do in order to begin school, play little league baseball, or get a driver's license: present a certified original of his or her birth certificate. Because he has not done this, President Obama appears to have something to hide, a fact that continues to undermine the most important earthly asset a president can have—the trust of the people.

It is an inconvenient question. Consequently, Obama and his supporters do not want to have to answer it. Instead, they brush the issue aside claiming it is nothing but the latest in a long line of conspiracy theories concocted by overly-imaginative wackos. No doubt this is an effective way to create a smoke-screen around the issue. After all, America certainly has its share of conspiracy theorists. But in the final analysis, this kind of response is likely to be viewed as just clever obfuscation, an approach that is likely to undermine public trust in a man who campaigned on transparency.

Some who believe that Obama is not an American citizen claim he was born in Kenya. Others believe that while living in Indonesia he became an Indonesian citizen. Still others believe that the President was born with dual citizenship—British and American—and, as a result, does not qualify as a *natural-born* citizen as prescribed in the United States Constitution. There are, no doubt, conspiracy theorists and people with a political axe to grind among those who question the President's citizenship. But there are also patriotic Americans who believe in full disclosure and are concerned about the same loyalty issues that guided the founders when they wrote Article II, Section 1, Clause 5 of the United States Constitution.

The Constitutional Issue

The controversy that began well before he was elected president centers around one simple question: Is Barack Obama a "natural born" citizen of the United States as required in Article II, Section 1, Clause 5 of the United States Constitution? This clause reads as follows:

> *No person except a natural-born Citizen, or a Citizen of the United States, at the time of the Adoption of this Constitution, shall be eligible to the office of President; neither shall any Person be eligible to that Office who shall not have attained the age of thirty-five years, and been fourteen Years a Resident within the United States.*

The controversy concerning President Obama's citizenship relates to the first part of Clause 5: "No person except a natural-born Citizen..." No one is claiming that Obama fails to comply with the part of the clause establishing thirty-five as the minimum age or that he has not been a resident of the United States for more than fourteen years.

Crux of the Constitutional Issue

Constitutional law is seldom simple and this is certainly the case when trying to decide if someone meets the qualifications to serve as President of the United States as specified in Article II, Section 1, Clause 5. For example, the following questions have arisen at various times in the past:

- What does it mean to be a "natural-born" citizen of the United States?

- In order to satisfy the "fourteen years" requirement in Clause 5, does an individual have to reside in the United States for fourteen consecutive years or can the total be cumulative?

- Does an individual have to reside in the United States the fourteen years immediately preceding his or her election to the presidency?

Fortunately, all of these questions and others like them have been dealt with in other cases. As a result, the crux of the issue now boils down to some simple questions that could be easily answered by a long-form birth certificate. In determining whether or not an individual is a "natural-born" citizen of the United States, there are several questions that must be answered including where he was born, when he was born, the nationalities of his parents, and where he lived with his parents.

Obama's mother was a natural-born United States citizen, but his father was a citizen of Kenya. Barack Obama, Sr. was not a United States citizen—natural-born or naturalized. This fact has given rise to some of the speculation that the President is not a United States citizen. The applicable law when Obama was born specified that if only one parent was a United States citizen at the time of his birth, that parent (Obama's mother) had to have resided in the United States for at least ten years. The law further stated that five of those ten years had to occur after the age of 16. Because Obama's mother was only eighteen at the time of his birth, she could not have resided in the United States for at least five years after her 16th birthday.[1]

Some doubters have used this fact about Obama's mother's age and the "five-year" requirement to back up their claims that the President is not a United States citizen. But those who do so are missing a key point. Whether Obama is or is not a United States citizen does not hang on this particular fact. That is unless Obama was, as many believe, born outside of the United States. The "five-year" requirement applies to those born outside of the United States.

There have been a number of other assertions made by doubters that, although interesting, are really just rabbit-trail issues. We believe that these often repeated assertions distract attention from the crux of the issue. In addition, some have been shown to be inaccurate. Rabbit-trail issues raised by doubters include:

• Barack Obama was originally named "Barry," his original middle name was Muhammed rather than Hussein, and his father was not Barack Obama, Sr. Even if these assertions turn out to be true, they do not disqualify the President as a United States citizen.

They might create a public-relations issue for him, but they would not nullify his citizenship.

- Obama could obtain a certificate of live birth from Hawaii's Department of Health without being born in Hawaii. This appears to be true, but the certificate of live birth would list his actual place of birth which would be someplace other than Hawaii, thereby defeating the purpose of the document from Obama's point of view.

- The President's grandmother has claimed that he was born in Africa. This is certainly interesting, but it amounts to hearsay. If the President can produce a proper birth certificate showing Hawaii as his birthplace, it will not matter what his grandmother said. If he cannot, the President still has a problem.

- Obama traveled to Pakistan at a time when there was a ban on U.S. passport holders entering that country. Consequently, he cannot be an American citizen. This is another issue that fails to prove the point even if he did make this trip since it could be explained away by inattentiveness on the part of Pakistani officials or any number of other explanations.

- There is no evidence that Obama's parents actually ever lived at the address given in a newspaper ad announcing his birth.

- Obama cannot be a United States citizen because even if he was born where he claims, Hawaii was not yet a state in 1961. This assertion is easily refuted since Hawaii became a state in 1959.

Assertions such as these, though interesting, are really just side issues that veer away from the real issue. We believe the appropriate approach for those who doubt the validity of President Obama's citizenship is to identify the crux of the issue and stay focused on it. Further, we believe that the crux of the Constitutional issue may be boiled down to one simple question: *Where was Barack Obama born?* If he can substantiate in an acceptable manner that he was, in fact, born in Hawaii, these side issues will not matter. If he cannot substantiate his citizenship, these side issues will become irrelevant.

Of course, no matter what happens there will always be conspiracy theorists who, for their own reasons, will continue to raise questions. But it is the concerned American citizen who, regardless of party affiliation, wants and needs to trust his President that is important here, not people who get their news from the tabloids and think Elvis is still alive. This is the crux of the issue, a fact that makes it all the more suspect when President Obama refuses to release a certified long-form original of his birth certificate. The danger Obama now faces is that how he handles the controversy will become more important than the actual birth certificate.

Why Does Obama's Citizenship Even Matter?

One of the reasons we decided to write this book is that people who should know better have asked why it even matters that President Obama be an American citizen. We find that those who have a *who-cares* attitude toward the issue fall into one of two categories: 1) those who do not understand why America's founders insisted that the President of the United States be a natural-born citizen, and 2) those who understand the concerns of the founders but think they are no longer relevant. Both groups would benefit from a brief seminar on the intentions of the founders in building the natural-born requirement into the Constitution.

Intent of the Founders in Article II, Section 1, Clause 5

The applicable clause reads in part, "No person except a natural-born Citizen...shall be eligible to the Office of President..." To the founders, the meaning of the term "natural-born" was self-evident—it required no explanation beyond that implicit in the term itself. Their reasoning in making this a requirement was also self-evident, at least to those present at the birth of our nation.

In specifying the natural-born requirement for those who would be president, the founders were guarding against what was a legitimate concern; the election of a president whose loyalty to another country would be stronger than his loyalty to the United States. We believe this concern is just as relevant now as it was then. The founders believed that someone born in the United States would naturally have a greater allegiance to this country than someone whose roots were elsewhere.

The founders understood the deep emotional pull one's birthplace can exert on an individual. They also understood the potentially disastrous ramifications of having a president whose allegiance to another country or system of government was stronger than his allegiance to the United States and its representative form of government. We do not believe that Americans should be any less concerned about these issues today than the founders were more than 230 years ago. If anything, we should be even more concerned.

Rightly or wrongly the founders' concern about a president's allegiance to the United States applies even more so in Obama's case than it has with his predecessors. We know that the President is smart enough to understand this whether he likes it or not. Consequently, we believe that he should have anticipated the issues his election would raise and gotten out in front of them by providing appropriate reassurances to the American people. It may not be fair, but it is fact that his Kenyan father, his Muslim-sounding name, his early years in Indonesia, and the time he spent under the mentorship of Frank Marshall Davis have caused many Americans to worry about his allegiance to the United States. Further, some of his statements and actions while in office—for example, apologizing for America and bowing to a Saudi Prince—have only served to increase the speculation about his mixed loyalties.

There are several reasons why many Americans find it difficult to trust that President Obama's highest allegiance is to the United States. First, there is the confusion surrounding his place of birth, which is further exacerbated by his father's nationality. Second, there is his Muslim-sounding name; an unfortunate coincidence at a time when there is so much tension and animosity between the United States and the Muslim world. Third, there are his seemingly anti-American statements made while on his various trips to foreign lands; trips that have come to be known as Obama's *apology tours*. This issue of trusting President Obama's allegiance to the United States is explored in greater detail in Chapter Three.

Obama's Handling of the Issue Fuels the Controversy

In 2007, Obama's campaign staff released an abstract of his *Certification of Live Birth*. Because this document does not qualify as an original birth certificate, it raised more questions than it answered. The President's refusal to go public with a certified original of his birth certificate has kept a controversy alive that most Americans think could be easily resolved unless

Obama does, in fact, have something to hide. Herein lies an issue even Obama's supporters struggle with. Like the doubters, even some of his supporters would like the President to put the issue to rest once and for all by simply producing the necessary document. So far this has not happened. In addition, he has sealed his college records and others that might provide insight into the issue.

One of the reasons the President's refusal to put this issue to rest has fanned the flames of controversy, is that most Americans can remember having to provide certified originals of their birth certificates on many different occasions. For example, the authors can remember having to provide certified originals of their birth certificates in order to enroll in school, play little league baseball, play high school football, get a driver's license, join the Marine Corps, and secure a pass to enter a military base. These are just a few occasions we can remember. There have, no doubt, been others. The question that disturbs many Americans about this controversy can be paraphrased as follows: If I have to provide a certified original of my birth certificate just to play little-league baseball, why shouldn't Barack Obama be required to produce one to be President of the United States?

Obama's Childhood Feeds the Controversy

Much of the controversy over the President's citizenship grows out of his somewhat murky childhood. According to the President, he was born at the Kapi'olani Medical Center in Honolulu, Hawaii. His mother was an American citizen from Wichita, Kansas named Ann Dunham. His father was a Kenyan citizen from Nyang'oma Kogelo, Nyanza Province named Barack Obama.[2] When Obama was two years old his father left the family.

Obama's birth parents divorced in 1964 and his mother later married Lolo Soetero, an Indonesian student attending the University of Hawaii. His new family moved to Indonesia—a Muslim country—in 1967. At this point, young Barack Obama became Barry Soetero and was given Indonesian citizenship. He attended public and private schools in Indonesia until the age of ten at which point he moved back to Hawaii to live with his maternal grandparents, Stanley and Madelyn Dunham.[3] It was while living in Hawaii with his maternal grandparents that Barack Obama (Barry Soetero) was introduced to Frank Marshall Davis, a communist activist, and came under his mentorship. This relationship and how it has contributed to the controversy is explored in Chapter Three.

Of course, the child who would become president had no control over the events of his early life. Like many children of divorce, he went where his parents took him and adjusted to the new circumstances as best he could. But the fact of a Kenyan father, the move to Indonesia, the return to Hawaii to live with his grandparents, and the mentoring he received from Frank Marshall Davis, have all been fodder for the speculation that has surrounded Barack Obama since he entered national politics—speculation he has steadfastly refused to clear up.

Some of the speculation that has grown out of President Obama's childhood is legitimate, some less so. However, fair or not, rumors that serve to undermine trust in this President continue to circulate because they have not been satisfactorily addressed. Most of these rumors could be easily set aside by producing a legitimate birth certificate.

Obama's Response Does Not Satisfy Doubters

Because the requirements to serve in Congress are less restrictive than those to serve as President, the birth-certificate controversy went mostly unnoticed by the American public until Barack Obama won the Democratic nomination and began campaigning for the presidency. Once the issue began to gain traction, he had to respond. The Obama campaign maintained a website called "Fight the Smears" that it used to counter politically-damaging questions and accusations leveled against the candidate.

In June 2007, the campaign posted the following message on this website, along with a scanned copy of a "Certification of Live Birth" from Hawaii's State Department of Health:

> Smears claiming Barack Obama doesn't have a birth certificate aren't actually about that piece of paper—they're about manipulating people into thinking Barack is not an American citizen. The truth is, Barack Obama was born in the state of Hawaii in 1961, a native citizen of the United States of America.[4]

Obama's supporters no doubt thought that this statement accompanied by the scanned image of a "Certification of Live Birth" would put the issue to rest. However, doubters were skeptical because they suspected that computer enhancements and alterations might have been made to the document. Other concerns raised by those who doubted the validity of the scanned copy were:

- Officials from Hawaii's Department of Health claimed that the original birth certificate had to be treated like that of any other citizen and so could not be released. This policy, of course, is fitting and proper. However, the Department of Health's response skirted the most important aspect of its policy: the original birth certificate could be released if its owner—the President of the United States—would give his permission.

- A *certification of live birth* does not qualify as a birth certificate. Rather, it is something known as a *short-form* certificate; a record that contains less information than the long-form certificate. It is this additional information in its original form that doubters want to see.

- Hawaii's Department of Health has steadfastly refused to confirm any information relating to the President's birth without Obama's permission. This, of course, is precisely the correct policy. But it only intensifies the skepticism since the President could simply sign the appropriate form and allow the complete story to be told.

We are less concerned about the validity of this document than we are about the fact that it is not a certified long-form birth certificate. This is the computer age. Documents are scanned all the time. Even the actual birth certificate might eventually be produced in scanned form. However, it should clearly be a scan of a vintage 1961 birth certificate that is certified to be an electronic version of the original.

Response of the President's Supporters to Doubters

In dealing with the controversy over President Obama's citizenship, his supporters have chosen to use the destructive *ad hominem* argument: *When debating an opponent, don't attack his arguments, attack him.* The theory behind the destructive *ad hominem* strategy is that the fastest and most effective way to undermine an opponent's point of view is to undermine the opponent's credibility. Using this approach, Obama's supporters have sought to discredit anyone who questions the President's citizenship. In the eyes of his supporters, to question the President on this issue is to be a conspiracy theorist, a disgruntled conservative who is a poor loser, or a racist who cannot countenance having an African-American in the Oval Office. Supported by an openly left-leaning press corps, Obama's supporters have been able to effectively label anyone who questions his citizenship in these derogatory ways.

The President's supporters have been aided and abetted in their campaign to malign doubters by a fringe element that does, in fact, hate the President and would like nothing more than to see him fail. For example, James Van Brunn, the gunman in the shooting at the Holocaust Memorial Museum in June 2009, was known to have posted Internet messages accusing the President of covering up the real facts surrounding his birth.[6]

The best way to discredit a group is to label it in a way that is new, catchy, and memorable. Knowing this, Obama's supporters have coined their own term for those who question the President's citizenship. They have given all doubters the label "birthers." Thus labeled, anyone who questions the president must be a wacko hooked on conspiracy theories who gets his news from the tabloids.

Interestingly, it is a liberal commentator who, despite her obvious distaste for those who question President Obama's place of birth, puts the issue in its proper perspective. Writing for *Salon*, feminist Camille Paglia makes an excellent point— one shared by the authors when you eliminate the name calling she indulges in to soften the blow of her recommendation to her fellow Obama supporters:

> I had thought for many months that the flap over Obama's birth certificate was a tempest in a teapot. But simple questions about the certificate were never resolved to my satisfaction. Thanks

to their own blathering, fanatical overkill, of course, the right-wing challenges to the birth certificate never gained traction. But Obama could have ended the entire matter months ago by publicly requesting Hawaii to issue a fresh, long-form, stamped certificate and inviting a few high-profile reporters in to examine the document and photograph it.[7]

We agree with Paglia but would suggest two pertinent revisions to her recommendation: 1) add some high-profile conservative commentators to the group to achieve an appropriate balance, and 2) ask Hawaii's Department of Health to produce the certified long-form rather than another computerized short-form.

Complaints of the Politically Expedient

Not all critics of doubters are liberals, Democrats, or Obama supporters. There are politically-expedient Republicans who think the controversy over the President's citizenship is a poorly-timed, ill-advised sideshow that distracts the Republican party from its focus on such issues as healthcare, energy policy, and global instability. In addition, some think that President Obama is purposely stringing out the controversy for his own political benefit. Those who take this line of reasoning think that the President and his supporters believe the controversy is hurting the credibility of the Republican Party and that the longer it continues the better it is for the Democrats.

The strongest criticism from the Right has come from well-known conservative commentator Michael Medved. Medved has been even more strident than Obama's supporters in attacking those who question the President's citizenship. He has called doubters "the worst enemy of the conservative movement" who make other conservatives look "sick, troubled and not suitable for civilized company."[8]

In responding to those who value political expedience over such issues as law, ethics, credibility, trust, transparency, and the ability to lead during difficult times, we encourage a second look at the situation. Politically expedient politicians are like the man who spends all his time straightening photographs on the wall of his den while his house is burning down. He has bigger issues to deal with, but refuses to acknowledge them.

In responding to Michael Medved's invective, we would encourage less heat and more light. While he is certainly within his rights to make these kinds of comments and accusations, this type of attack does little to encourage reasonable dialogue at a time when reasonable dialogue is badly needed. The issues concerning the validity of the President's citizenship as well as his credibility, trustworthiness, transparency, and ability to lead are worthy of a higher level of debate than will be achieved by mean-spirited name calling.

Legal and Political Action Resulting from the Controversy

At this writing, the birth certificate issue has gained little or no traction in the national media, liberal or conservative. On CNN, a liberal news network, commentator Lou Dobbs was taken to task by the president of the network for suggesting that President Obama should produce his birth certificate. Dobbs did not question Obama's citizenship. Rather, he questioned the President's refusal to verify it. On Fox News, a conservative news network, commentator Bill O'Reilly proclaimed Obama an American citizen. Clearly, the national media is either not interested in the controversy or is interested in suppressing it.

However, at the grass roots level it is a different story. Numerous individuals and groups have filed lawsuits in an attempt to compel President Obama to produce conclusive proof of his citizenship. In addition, state legislatures have begun to take action relating to the controversy. These facts are evidence of grassroots interest that could grow and become a problem, first for members of Congress and, if this happens, for the President.

Lawsuits Filed Against the President

Lawsuits have been filed by individuals in Connecticut, Hawaii, Texas, Ohio, New Jersey, Pennsylvania, North Carolina, and the state of Washington that either challenge Barack Obama's eligibility to serve as President or seek to compel him to provide conclusive proof of his American citizenship. These lawsuits, although indicative of a lack of grassroots trust in the President, have had little effect because, to date, they have all been dismissed, primarily on the grounds of insufficient standing.

Standing is a legal concept that requires the plaintiff in a civil lawsuit to show he has suffered harm by the actions of the person he is suing. So far, the courts have consistently determined that the plaintiffs in lawsuits brought against President Obama have lacked the standing necessary to give their lawsuits validity. Judge R. Barclay Surrick of the United States District Court for the Eastern District of Pennsylvania, one of the judges who has dismissed a lawsuit filed against the President, explained his rationale for doing so by comparing the level of harm Obama's election might have caused to an individual citizen with that citizen's ability to derail the democratic process by filing a lawsuit. In Judge Surrick's view, individual American voters cannot claim to have suffered sufficient personal harm to undo an election in which millions of others participated and do not feel harmed.[9]

Suing—not just this president but any President of the United States—is a dead end street from a legal perspective and from the perspective of the democratic process. If the President—regardless of who that person happens to be at a given time—can be sued, every person who has a grievance of any kind against the President is going to sue. In this scenario, the office of the President would soon be overwhelmed by the volume of lawsuits it had to deal with, and the presidency would be neutered by the legal system. Although this might appeal to those who disagree with a given president, it is well to remember that the shoe could be on the other foot after the next election.

Birth Certificates Produced by Others

The Obama campaign staff is not the only entity to produce a document in an attempt to resolve the citizenship controversy. The certification of live birth produced during the presidential campaign was provided by Obama's staffers in an attempt to answer the inconvenient question that kept popping up. Of course, the certification of live birth—often referred to as the short-form birth certificate—did little to answer the questions of doubters. In fact, it instigated a whole new line of questioning.

Doubters have also had their share of misfires during the controversy. Several bogus birth certificates showing Obama's birthplace as Kenya have been circulated on the Internet, but were quickly shown to be fraudulent. However, an attorney in California—Orly Taitz—produced a document that he claims is a valid Kenyan birth certificate showing that Obama was born on August 4, 1961 in Coast General Hospital in Mombasa, Kenya. This document lists the mother as Stanley Ann Obama, formerly Stanley Ann Dunham, and the father as Barack Hussein Obama.[10]

Obama supporters immediately discounted this document as a forgery and a fraud. The main issue raised by the Obama camp was the date of the document: February 17, 1964. The "Certified Copy of Registration of Birth" is an official document of the Republic of Kenya (if it is real). Obama supporters claimed that Kenya did not become a republic until December 1964. However, official records show that the Kenyan independence movement actually began in 1957 and independence was achieved in 1963. As of this writing, Taitz had filed a motion in U.S. District Court for authentication of his document.[11]

State Legislation Resulting from the Controversy

Several state legislatures—Missouri, Oklahoma, Tennessee—have considered bills attempting to require candidates for public office to show proof of their citizenship. These bills have fared no better than the lawsuits filed against President Obama by private citizens. However, like the lawsuits, they are evidence of grassroots dissatisfaction with how the President is handling the controversy. If President Obama's approval rating continues to drop, support for state legislation is likely to increase.

The lawsuits filed against President Obama, as well as the bills filed in state legislatures, have little significance in the courts of the land, but they might have enormous significance in the court of public opinion—a court to which every president must answer. Although the various media outlets have chosen to either ignore the birth-certificate controversy or give it only passing attention, there is evidence of a rising tide of dissent at the grass roots level, and Obama's supporters in Congress are beginning to take notice. This is the significance of the lawsuits filed against the President and bills filed in state legislatures.

If those members of Congress who must run for office during the President's first term become convinced that his obfuscation in handling the controversy is threatening their reelections, the pressure on the President to put an end to it will only increase. If his approval rating continues to drop, the standing of President Obama's doubters in the court of public opinion will increase. This fact makes one of the key points that we will emphasize throughout this book. In the final analysis, it will be how Americans interpret President Obama's response to the birth-certificate controversy and not the mysterious birth certificate itself that will determine the outcome of this controversy. He may be able to avoid giving doubters their day in federal court, but if his approval ratings continue to drop because Americans feel they cannot trust him, President Obama will not be able to escape an eventual day of reckoning in the court of public opinion.

NOTES

1. "Is Barack Obama a natural-born citizen of the U.S.? Retrieved from www.snopes.com/politics/obama/citizen.asp on July 21, 2009.

2. Barack Obama, *Dreams from My Father: A Story of Race and Inheritance* (New York, NY: Three Rivers Press, 1995).

3. Ibid.

4. "The Truth About Barack's birth certificate." Retrieved from http://fightthesmears.com/articles/5/birthcertificate on November 15, 2008.

5. Rachel Maddow, "The Rachel Maddow Show," MSNBC, aired March 13, 2009.

6. Ben Smith, "Shooter was a Birther." Retrieved from www.politico.com/blogs/bensmith/0609/Shooter_was_a_Birther.html on June 10, 2009.

7. Camille Paglia, "Obama surfs through." *Salon*, November 12,

2008.

8. Greg Victor, "New Ideas, Sharp Opinions," *Pittsburgh Post-Gazette*, March 8, 2009.

9.   Jeff Bravin, "Why Some Constitutional Suits Don't Stand a Chance in Court," *Wall Street Journal.* Retrieved from http://online.wsj.com/article/SB123440666520775795.html on February 13, 2009.

10. WorldNetDaily. "Is this really smoking gun of Obama's Kenyan birth?" Retrieved from http://www.wnd.com/index.php?fa=PAGE.view&pageId=105764 on August 3, 2009.

11. Ibid.

TWO

Is There Room for Reason?

Few presidents have generated so much controversy so early in their administrations as Barack Obama. There is the birth certificate issue, healthcare, climate control, world instability, and, of course, the economy. If he succeeds at nothing else, Barack Obama has certainly been effective at creating political debate. Add to these issues the questions of transparency and broken promises that continue to swirl around President Obama and the controversy only gets worse.

Certainly the presidency has seen its share of controversies over the years. The pardoning of Richard Nixon by Gerald Ford, Jimmy Carter's Iranian hostage crisis, Ronald Reagan's Iran-Contra affair, George H. W. Bush's failed *read-my-lips* promise, Bill Clinton's impeachment and various other imbroglios, and George W. Bush's first election all generated their share of venom from the press and public.

But Barack Obama's birth-certificate controversy, coupled with questions of transparency and trust, might just set a record for the amount of vitriol, invective, and mean-spirited rhetoric it is generating from both predictable sources, as well as a few surprising ones. One of the reasons the volume surrounding the birth-certificate/transparency controversy is even louder than that of other presidential controversies is the internet. Blogs have enabled so many more people to speak their minds and have their voices heard. This is certainly happening in the debate over the President's citizenship and trustworthiness, which is another reason why the Left-leaning national media has been unable to effectively defuse or suppress the debate.

To many on the Left, those who doubt the validity of President Obama's American citizenship or question his transparency are nothing more than addle-brained conspiracy-theorists, a group the Left has labeled "birthers." To some on the Right, doubters are distracting Americans from more important issues such as healthcare, energy, and global instability, and are giving the President a way to drive a wedge between moderate and conservative Republicans. In other words, to critics on the Left, one must be a conspiracy wacko to question the President's citizenship and to some in the Republican ranks, one must be an idealist who is indifferent to the need for political expedience.

Several other motives have been attributed to doubters including political sour grapes, addiction to conspiracy theories, and an inability to accept that America has elected its first African-American president. If you listen to the noisy invective from the Left, coupled with pleas for political expedience from some on the Right, it is easy to wonder if there is any room for reason in the debate.

Must one be a conspiracy-theorist to be concerned about the validity of the President's citizenship or to point out his broken promises? Must one be a racist in order to question his trustworthiness? Is political expedience really more important than a major Constitutional issue? Does the fact that some conspiracy theorists question the President's citizenship mean that all who question it are like-minded? Does the fact that some who doubt the validity of Obama's claims of transparency are politically motivated mean that all who doubt them are also politically motivated? We don't think so. In fact, we think there are reasonable people who sincerely care about the Constitutional, ethical, legal, political, transparency, and leadership issues raised by the controversies surrounding this president. This is why we decided to write this book.

As we read more and more about the questions surrounding President Obama's birth certificate and his broken promise of transparency, we noticed that the attacks on doubters had become especially shrill and even mean-spirited. As we contemplated this fact, we were reminded of what Thomas Jefferson's political nemesis, John Marshall—later to become Chief Justice of the U.S. Supreme Court—once said when asked about those who questioned the controversial Alien and Sedition Acts: "I do not think them fraught with all those mischiefs which many gentlemen ascribed to them."[1]

This is how we came to see many of those who question President Obama's citizenship and trustworthiness. Although we do not deny that some of the doubters have less than pristine motives, we believe that painting them all with the same broad brush is both inaccurate and unfair. Many of the doubters appear to be reasonable, intelligent Americans who are appropriately concerned about what could become a major Constitutional crisis.

As we studied this issue, we certainly came across those who were glad to have a juicy new conspiracy theory to chew on. And yes, there were those who would gladly undo the Obama presidency for reasons of bias or political sour grapes. However, there were also voices of reason being raised to ask thoughtful questions that we believe are legitimate and need to be explored. Among these reasonable voices there are even a few belonging to Obama's supporters.

The obvious question, of course, has to do with whether or not President Obama meets the citizenship requirements set forth in Article II, Section 1, Clause 5 of the United States Constitution. The other questions typically grow out of how the

President and his supporters have responded to the first question. These include:

- Are the First Amendment rights of doubters being suppressed through pressure, browbeating, threats, or intimidation?

- Is President Obama behaving like the *transparent* president he promised to be—can he be trusted?

- Can President Obama lead the country out of the current economic quagmire without first earning the trust of the American people?

- Aside from whether or not President Obama was an American at birth, is he an American at heart?

In this book, we explore these questions and offer our thoughts concerning the answers to them. Throughout, we attempt to bring the voice of reason to a debate that we believe represents one of the most important political and legal issues in the history of our country. The controversy over President Obama's citizenship raises some important and inconvenient questions that many would like to either ignore or just see go away. However, in a democratic society it is often the types of questions that we least want to confront that are most deserving of our attention. We believe this is the case with the question of President Obama's citizenship, as well as with how he chooses to respond to the question.

Why the Questions Must Be Asked and Answered

Perhaps the kindest label that has been attached to those who question the validity of President Obama's citizenship is *conspiracy theorist*. Other terms that have been used include *crazy, nutburger, demagogue, exploitive, irresponsible,* and—our favorite—*filthy conservative imposter*. Clearly, to question the President's citizenship or trustworthiness is to incur the wrath of the Left, as well as a few on the Right. The clear implication is that only a wacko would ask such inconvenient questions.

This is unfortunate because, in spite of claims to the contrary, the questions do raise a serious Constitutional issue and the President's response to it raises other issues (*e.g.* trust, credibility, transparency, and the ability to lead). Further, even if there are those with self-serving motives who question the President's citizenship and trustworthiness, there are also appropriately concerned American citizens who have a right to expect a more definitive answer from a president who campaigned on a promise of transparency.

We suggest that there are several big-picture issues that transcend the objections of those who wish to sweep the citizenship question under the rug. These issues grow out of the citizenship question itself, as well as the President's response to it, and are even more important than the political, cultural, and racial vindication that Obama supporters feel they achieved with his election to the presidency. The big-picture issues that concern us are:

- The obvious Constitutional issue. The Constitution is the law of the land, it is the foundation of all of the other laws that American citizens are expected to obey every day. As the leader of our nation, the

President must set a consistent example of complying with the Constitution. If he simply ignores the law of the land, American citizens will begin to wonder why they are not allowed to ignore the law too. When this happens in a nation of laws, the very structure of society begins to break down. Those who argue that the "natural-born" element of the Constitution should be ignored in Obama's case, so as to erase a long-standing stain on America's conscience, are just arguing that we should trade one wrong for another. They are saying that the end justifies the means. What they fail to realize is that this end—if achieved in violation of the Constitution— will undermine the document that is the foundation of America's liberty.

- The credibility of Obama's presidency and the presidency itself are at stake. As to Obama's presidency, he ran on a platform of transparency. He claimed that he would be a president that Americans could trust. Yet when asked to verify his citizenship—something that all Americans are asked to do numerous times in their lives—the President responded in a way that, rightly or wrongly, gives the appearance of a cover-up. Further, before becoming president, Obama took an oath of Office in which he said: "I do solemnly swear that I will faithfully execute the Office of the President of the United States, and will, to the best of my Ability, preserve, protect, and defend the Constitution of the United States." You do not preserve, protect, or defend the Constitution by violating one of its most basic requirements. In order to lead, one must have credibility with his followers. In order to enjoy the asset of credibility, a leader must first earn the trust of his followers. People will not follow those they do not trust. Obfuscation about his place of birth may be effective political spin, but it will not win the trust of American citizens. If Americans come to believe that there is one set of standards for them and another for the President of the United States when it comes to obeying the law, they will eventually lose their trust in the office itself and in the law. If this happens, the seeds of America's destruction as a democratic republic will have been sown.

- The democratic process itself is threatened by the response of the Left as well as a few politically-expedient conservatives. Political dissent is one of the most fundamental of our nation's freedoms. Americans must be able to question their elected officials without fear of intimidation or threat. This is especially true when the elected official is the President of the United States. George Orwell had it right when he said: "If liberty means anything at all, it means the right to tell people what they don't want to hear."[2] By logical extension, it also means the right to ask inconvenient questions. We believe that this aspect of the controversy is so important that even if all doubters were conspiracy-theorists or disgruntled voters, their First-Amendment rights should still be respected and protected. Doubters are not all conspiracy buffs and sore losers, of course. However, even if this were the case, our conviction would still stand. If we have come to the point in America where the historical ramifications of an election trump the First-Amendment rights of American citizens, we have started down the slippery slope to totalitarianism. The response of President Obama and his supporters to townhall meetings conducted across the United States in August 2009 suggest that raising the frightening specter of totalitarianism is not to exaggerate. Obama's supporters in the United States Senate were sent on a mission during the summer break: go home and sell the President's healthcare initiative to an increasingly doubtful American public. The sales job flopped. In fact, it backfired. Everyday Americans clearly vocalized their concerns and expressed their disapproval. The Obama administration responded by calling these American citizens nothing but "angry mobs." The President, who told dissenters in essence to "shut up," also sent out a call to supporters to attend the townhall meetings and show their support for his healthcare plan. In one meeting, the Obama crowd showed its support by physically beating a dissenter.

Taking all of these facts into account, we believe that those who are concerned about the validity of President Obama's citizenship and trustworthiness, should be able to ask their questions and expect to have them answered satisfactorily. To do so is to apply the most fundamental principles of freedom and liberty, principles upon which our country was founded. We encourage those who disagree to step back from the political fray, think more cross-generationally into the future, and decide if the reasons behind your opposition are more important than the credibility of the president you support, the First-Amendment rights of all American citizens, the long-term viability of the presidency, and the founding principles without which our country would cease to exist as the world's last great bastion of freedom and liberty.

A Word of Caution for Doubters

Having researched the birth-certificate controversy thoroughly, we feel compelled to state that we do not believe that the Congress or the Courts have the political will to force the President to produce a valid birth certificate. Worse yet, we do not believe that they have the political will to remove him from office, even if they learn conclusively that Barack Obama is not an American citizen. This is a sad assertion, but we believe it is accurate. For those Americans concerned about the legal, ethical, transparency, and leadership issues this controversy has generated, our assertion may be a bitter pill to swallow. We certainly do not like what this assertion says about our country.

However, if you find our assertion disturbing—and you should—remember this: the end of the story has not yet been written. We believe this controversy will eventually be resolved, but not in Congress or the Courts. We believe it will be resolved in the court of public opinion. We predict that President Obama will eventually fail in this arena because the American people will lose trust in a president who campaigned on a platform of transparency and has steadfastly refused to be transparent on an issue as important as his citizenship.

NOTES

1. Jeffrey Rosen, *The Supreme Court: The Personalities and Rivalries That Defined America*, (New York, NY: Time Books, 2006), 50.

2. George Orwell, as quoted in *Closed Minds? Politics and ideology in American Universities* by A. Lee Fritschler, Bruce L. R. Smith, and Jeremy D. Mayer, as presented in "Civic Education, Not Right or Left Education," Jack Miller Center. Retrieved from http://www.jackmillercenter. org on January 3, 2009.

THREE

Why is President Obama Not Trusted?

*"The American people have legitimate fears
about where this country is headed and what it
means for their future and the future
of their children."*
U. S. Representative Charlie Melancon of Louisiana
Washington Times, July 20, 2009

President Obama fares best in the realm of broad philosophical generalities. It is when the details of his beliefs,
programs, and policies are revealed that problems arise. These
problems relate to credibility and trust, a fact that bodes poorly
for the President. Few things are more essential to effective
leadership than trust. Trust is difficult to earn but easy to lose.
A leader can lose the trust of his followers simply on the basis of
suspicion. Leaders face the challenge of persuading their followers to go where they might not yet be ready to go. In Obama's
case this means persuading an American public that agreed
with Ronald Reagan's belief that government is the problem to
suddenly reverse course and accept that government has now
become the solution. Even with the desperation induced by a
faltering economy and the assistance of a left-leaning media,
this has been a tough sell for President Obama.

The President is trying to lead the American public in a direction it finds increasingly suspect. He got a good head start
in the wrong direction because of: 1) economic desperation
on Wall Street and Main Street, 2) the media-assisted attacks

on George W. Bush, and 3) the honeymoon enjoyed by all new presidents. But now that the dust of historical significance and racial vindication has begun to settle and the details of his programs and policies have begun to surface, many Americans are putting on the brakes. As of this writing, President Obama's approval rating is dropping steadily. In fact, there appears to be a direct correlation between how much the American public learns about his big-government, socialistic programs and how fast his approval rating drops. The message is clear: President Obama has a trust problem, a problem that is aggravated by one of his favorite concepts—change.

Leadership, Trust, and Change

Much of leadership is about change. In order to make things better, leaders must be able to change the status quo. Having a vision for improvement—making things better for followers—and then being able to convince followers to do what is necessary to achieve the vision, is one of the fundamental challenges faced by all leaders in a democratic society. This is why it is so important for leaders to win the confidence and trust of those they wish to follow them. Winning the trust of followers is always a challenge for new leaders, and change makes the challenge even more difficult to overcome.

Before getting into the specifics of how all of this applies to President Obama, we will present some background information on what leaders who propose major changes must do if they are going to succeed. Then we will compare this with how President Obama is handling the birth-certificate controversy, as well as his promise to the American public to be a transparent president. Because neither the courts nor the Congress seem to have the will to compel President Obama to clear up the controversy over his citizenship, it is these issues of transparency and trust that are most likely to be Obama's undoing in the court of public opinion.

Don't Just Change—Improve

Few topics receive more attention in leadership literature than change. There are those who advocate change for the sake of change. This philosophy is best exemplified by the book, *If It Ain't Broke...Break It!* by Robert J. Kriegel and Louis Patler. Then there are those at the other end of the spectrum who think the world needs to slow down and stop changing. This philosophy is best exemplified by the book, *Calling a Halt to Mindless Change* by John MacDonald.

We believe that both of these philosophies are wrong. When it comes to winning support for change, leaders need to understand that their followers will go along only if they think the change will result in improvement. The most successful leaders understand that they cannot just change the circumstances of their followers, they must improve them. Leaders must be able to show that they are going to improve the lives and circumstances of their followers.

Inherent Discomfort of People with Change

It is a basic characteristic of human nature that people form psychological attachments to the familiar. We all have a natural human penchant for becoming comfortable with sameness. In a world of uncertainty, people find comfort in the familiar and reassurance in the predictable. There is nothing new in this. Even in bygone eras when change happened more slowly than it does now, people were prone to resist change. "Resistance to change is not a modern concept. In fact, resistance to change seems to have endured through the ages, in part because humans are biologically hard-wired to resist change. Yes, that's right. We are programmed not to change...we are wired to survive, so we hang on to what has worked in the past."[1]

As we show later in this chapter, natural human reluctance to change is a potential stumbling block for a leader such a President Obama who: 1) by virtue of being the first African-American president represents change of historical magnitude, and 2) campaigned on the promise of change, albeit unspecified change, but change nonetheless.

Can President Obama Overcome the Growing Discomfort with his Proposed Changes?

Leaders who hope to win broad-based support among their followers for the changes they hope to make must do at least the following:

- Establish a cogent and compelling vision for change

- Communicate the change vision to all stakeholders

- Win the trust of stakeholders so they will commit to supporting the proposed change

We contend that President Obama has failed to accomplish any of these three essential steps. Two key planks in his campaign platform were transparency and change. However, beginning with the birth-certificate controversy and spreading to all aspects of his administration, President Obama has been anything but transparent. Further, his vision for change is neither cogent nor compelling. Rather, it is fuzzy and ever-changing. The American people elected him without bothering to pin him down about the specifics of his change vision, and without any help in this regard from a left-leaning press corps. Now that they are learning the specifics, many Americans do not like what they see. In fact, what they are belatedly learning about Obama's vision for change is downright frightening.

President Obama has failed to win sufficient trust among the American people to gain their support for his change vision. The more Americans learn about the details of his major policy changes in the areas of foreign policy, healthcare, energy policy, the environment, and economic policy, the less they trust him. A major part of why he is not trusted by so many is how he has chosen to handle the birth-certificate controversy after promising to be a transparent president. Going back on promises is one of the most detrimental things a leader can do if he hopes to win and maintain trust. Just ask George H. W. Bush what happens when you promise "no new taxes" and then raise taxes. This single broken promise, more than any other factor, cost him a second term in the White House. Breaking his promise about transparency and not just as it relates to the birth-certificate controversy might eventually be the undoing of Obama's presidency.

Although we do not necessarily agree with them because the Constitutional issue is paramount, many Americans believe that his handling of the controversy is even more important than what the missing birth certificate might actually say. This growing unrest with President Obama's lack of transparency, coupled with the unwillingness of Congress and the courts to compel him to properly document his citizenship is why we believe the birth-certificate controversy will eventually be settled in the court of public opinion. Further, we believe that this court will eventually rule against Obama.

Why an Increasing Number of Americans Do Not Trust President Obama

Ask Americans if they like President Obama and you get one answer. Ask if they trust him and you get a different answer. Obama's backtracking is having the same effect as George H.W. Bush's backtracking—a loss of credibility. In fact, an AOL poll of more than 30,000 people released by WorldNetDaily in July 2009 showed that 82 percent of respondents want President Obama to release his birth certificate.[2] This poll supports our contention that although the media, Congress, and the courts have chosen to ignore or downplay the controversy, in the court that will ultimately rule on the issue—the court of public opinion—interest is substantial and growing.

In the remainder of this chapter, we summarize some of the reasons why an increasing number of Americans do not trust President Obama. Our point in presenting this information is that there will be a day of reckoning concerning the President's citizenship and broken promises. America is a nation of laws, and the Constitution is still the law of the land. No person in America is above the law, and this includes the President of the United States, regardless of the historic significance of his election. The media, Congress, and courts can postpone President Obama's inevitable day of reckoning, but the American people will tire of broken promises and cleverly-worded political spin. When this happens, they will make the final decision about Obama's citizenship, his presidency, and his legacy.

Trust and the Healthcare Issue

The most substantial and far-reaching change President Obama has proposed is nationalization of the healthcare industry. Having seen the Clinton administration's attempts to provide universal healthcare shot down in flames, Obama knew he was facing an uphill battle. He knew that Americans were fearful of the effect his proposal would have on the quality of healthcare, the nation's budget, and their personal finances. To alleviate these fears, candidate Obama promised complete transparency as the issue was discussed and debated.

Here is what he said: "I'm going to have all of the negotiations around a big table. We'll have doctors and nurses and hospital administrators. Insurance companies, drug companies they'll get a seat at the table, they just won't be able to buy every chair. But what we will do is, we'll have the negotiations televised on C-SPAN, so that people can see who is making arguments on behalf of their constituents, and who are making arguments on behalf of the drug companies or the insurance companies."[3]

The problem is that the debate around the big table has not occurred on C-SPAN or anywhere else. Only when he could not get his healthcare initiative passed, did President Obama send emissaries out across America in an attempt to generate grass roots support—a strategy that backfired badly from the outset. Matters only got worse when Obama's supporters referred to American citizens who expressed concern about the healthcare initiative as "mobs." Further, when a watchdog group—Citizens for Responsibility and Ethics in Washington—asked to see White House visitor logs to determine if healthcare executives had visited to discuss the issue off line, the Obama administration refused to honor their request. This is not just a lack of transparency, it is a cover up. According to Alex Koppelman, "the Obama administration is still adopting legal positions about executive power and secrecy that the president said he opposed when he was campaigning."[4] The issue of saying one thing during the campaign and doing another once elected is becoming a common theme in the debates about President

Obama's transparency. The net result of this type of political two-step is an erosion of trust in the President.

President Obama has been his own worst enemy in trying to win support for his healthcare proposals because his conflicting public statements have created an air of mistrust. To begin with, Obama's claim that government can operate the nation's healthcare system more efficiently than the private sector is counter-intuitive to Americans who have never seen government do anything efficiently. Pertinent questions have been asked by people who are well-informed about healthcare, and Obama has answered them, but his answers seem to vary from day to day. Further, his most recent answers do not square with what he promised during his presidential campaign. Questions that have received a mixed bag of answers include the following:

- Will the proposed healthcare system cover all Americans?

- Will the healthcare system lower costs in the private and public sectors over the long-term or drive them ever higher?

- Will the quality of healthcare improve or decline under the proposed system?

- Will people lose their healthcare because of pre-existing conditions?

- Will people be able to opt out of the system?

- Will the system emphasize prevention and wellness?

- Will people be able to retain the physicians who are treating them now?

- Will the government have to continually raise taxes
  to pay for the system?

All of these are good questions, but the same cannot be said about President Obama's answers—partly because it is so hard to pin down his answers. Saying one thing during the campaign and another after he is elected gives the President the appearance of a politician who will say anything to get elected, but will not follow through on his promises. Varying his answers from day to day gives him the appearance of a President who has not adequately thought through his proposal. This, of course, is no way to build trust, and trust is President's Obama's Achilles heel.

Trust and Taxes

During his campaign for the presidency, Obama vowed continually that he would not raise taxes, except on the wealthiest Americans (as if the fact of their wealth somehow makes raising taxes any less loathsome or more just). In this case, the waffling and political sleight-of-hand began even before the campaign was over. Obama and his campaign staff changed their minds continually over the income level that would be applied in deciding if an individual taxpayer was considered wealthy.

Like his healthcare proposal, candidate Obama's tax proposal sounded counter-intuitive. When he claimed that he would cut taxes for 95 percent of Americans, the numbers just did not add up. Doug Holtz-Eakin, commenting on this phenomenon, said:

> They have said so many things throughout the
> campaign. It is clear that Barack Obama on taxes
> will say anything that is politically expedient
> including I will cut taxes for 95% of Americans.

The fact is he has promised so much spending
it would be impossible for those tax cuts to take
place. He has proposed over $800 billion worth
of increases in spending that excludes a recent
independent estimate of his healthcare plan
which would cost over $240 billion a year alone.
It is an inconceivable matter of arithmetic in
modern financial markets that he could cut
taxes and follow through on the spending
promises he made. There is no credibility in
this package.[5]

This comment was made during the presidential campaign.
We now know that the estimates on increased spending and
the cost of Obama's healthcare proposal provided during the
campaign were astoundingly low.

Now that reality is setting in concerning America's ability to pay for Obama's healthcare program, stimulus package,
bailouts, and various other handouts and entitlements, he is
backtracking on the tax issue. Many Americans see this as the
epitome of arrogance. After promising to not raise taxes on
anyone who earned less than $250,000 per year (although this
amount changed several times during the presidential campaign), Obama was not even eight months into his presidency
before he began saying that the American middle-class might
have to be taxed at a higher rate to pay for his big-government,
socialistic programs. Even though President George H.W. Bush
lost out on a second term because he broke his promise of no
new taxes, President Obama appears to be arrogant enough to
assume that he deserves a pass for doing the same thing.

Broken promises, estimates that appear to be purposefully
and knowingly low, and obfuscation on taxes together are just
one more reason so many Americans are coming to the conclu-

sion they cannot trust President Obama. As mistrust over his policies, proposals, and promises grows, the pressure to come clean about his citizenship will also grow, if not in Congress and the courts, then in the court of public opinion.

Trust and the Issue of Race

One of the great hopes of those who voted for Barack Obama was that he would bridge the racial gap that still exists in America. Thomas Sowell wrote this in his syndicated column:

> Many people hoped that the election of a black President of the United States would mark our entering in "post-racial" era, when we could finally put some ugly aspects of our history behind us. That is quite understandable. But it takes two to tango. Those of us who want to see racism on its way out need to realize that others benefit greatly from crying racism. They benefit politically, financially, and socially.[6]

Sowell makes the point that for years Barack Obama has aligned himself with people who benefit from perpetuating racism. "He found it expedient to appeal to a wider electorate as a post-racial candidate, just as he found it expedient to say a lot of other popular things—about campaign finance, about transparency in government, about not rushing legislation through Congress without having it first posted on the Internet long enough to be studied—all of which turned out to be the direct opposite of what he actually did after getting elected."[7]

Sowell puts his finger on how Obama has gotten away with the obvious contradictions between his words and actions. Too many people view him through the lens of how they want things to be, rather than how they really are. For example, how could Americans, familiar with Barack Obama's twenty-year association with the Reverend Jeremiah Wright and his racially-explosive ranting, profess to be shocked when the President, without first bothering to get the facts, automatically sided with Harvard professor Henry Louis Gates, calling the actions of Cambridge police "stupid"? [8]

The incident in question occurred in July 2009. Gates, just home from a trip, was having trouble getting into his house. His front door was stuck and he had to use his shoulder to knock it open. To a neighbor his actions looked like those of someone breaking into a house, so she called the Cambridge police. When the police responded to the call, words were exchanged between the upset Gates and the investigating officer. His immediate reaction was to cry "racial profiling" and subject the investigating officer to a loud, sustained tirade full of invective. As a result, Gates found himself handcuffed and carted off to jail for a brief stay. President Obama's immediate reaction was to join Gates in his tirade and make it a chorus, declaring that the police had acted "stupidly."

When the dust settled and the facts were sorted out, it was determined that the officer in charge had responded properly to a 911 call and that the issue was one of public safety, not racism or racial profiling. An embarrassed President, seeing the position his kneejerk reaction had put him in, called a news conference and made a concerted effort to do what he has become noted for—using carefully scripted words to undo those spoken in haste without a script. Although he tried hard to distract public attention away from his ill-considered comments—for example, using the ploy of inviting Gates and the arresting officer to the White House for a beer—it was glaringly obvious to the American public that something was missing in the President's condescending rhetoric: an actual apology. A colleague of one of the authors spoke for many Americans when he said, "Obama's not sorry for what he said. He's sorry that he got caught with his foot in his mouth and that his friends in the media could not bail him out."

In the immediate aftermath of the Cambridge incident, questions began to surface that only serve to undermine the trust of the American people in a president who badly needs to earn their trust. Perhaps the most pertinent question was: Why would a President of the United States even involve himself in a routine local police matter? Thomas Sowell answered this question with his characteristic succinctness and accuracy: "The racial profiling issue is a great vote getter. And if it polarizes the society, that is a price that politicians are willing to pay in order to get votes. Academics who run black studies departments, as Professor Henry Louis Gates does, likewise have a vested interest in racial paranoia."[9]

Other questions that surfaced in the aftermath of the Cambridge incident also bode poorly for President Obama from the perspective of winning public trust. These questions include the following:

- Why didn't President Obama do the courageous thing and issue a simple, straight-forward, sincere apology to the Cambridge Police Department?

- Why would President Obama jump to the conclusion that racial profiling was behind the arrest of Gates without even bothering to first get all of the facts?

- Has President Obama exchanged the issue of racism for racialism?

Speaking practically, President Obama missed a great opportunity with the Cambridge incident. Actually, he missed two opportunities. The first one he missed was the opportunity to simply stay out of the matter and let it be handled by the local police for what it was—a routine response to a 911 call. The second one he missed was the opportunity to look straight into the camera and apologize to the American public, the Cambridge Police Department, and the officer who responded. If he were a better student of American history, this is precisely what he would have done.

Even a History 101 student could have told the President that the most popular moment in the brief tenure of one of his predecessors in the Oval Office was when he called a news conference, accepted responsibility for a major blunder, and apologized to the American people. When President John F. Kennedy accepted responsibility for the Bay of Pigs debacle and apologized to the American public, his approval rating shot through the roof. Americans respect and can relate to a president who has the courage to say, "I made a mistake and I apologize."

As to why President Obama would jump to the conclusion that racial profiling was behind the arrest of Professor Gates, Thomas Sowell has already answered this question. However, the question about substituting racialism for racism is worthy of exploring. When President Obama assumed that racial profiling was behind the arrest of Professor Gates, he was practicing the concept of racialism, not racism.

Trust and the Concept of Racialism

When President Obama condemned the actions of the Cambridge police without first getting the facts, he was practicing a concept known as *racialism*. Racialism is not racism, which is hatred of or bias against another race. Rather, it consists of viewing the world through the lens of race, forming opinions and making decisions on the basis of race. Racialism is a presuppositional way of viewing the world that can result in false assumptions. For example, in the case of the Cambridge police incident involving Professor Gates, President Obama assumed that the police were engaging in racial profiling, rather than simply responding to a routine 911 call. Making this assumption without first getting the facts is an example of racialism.

Assume that a white person sits down to have lunch in a Mexican restaurant and the waiter is Hispanic. The waiter is rude and the service is poor. If the customer assumes that the waiter is being rude because he dislikes white people, he is practicing racialism. After all, the waiter could just be having a bad day or maybe he is just a rude person who should find another line of work. To assume that the issue in question is related to race without knowing more about the situation is to practice racialism. Racialism is not so heinous a concept as racism, but neither is it commendable. As a practice, it is certainly beneath the dignity of an American president, especially one who was going to help close the racial gap in this country.

In her excellent book, *Finding Soul Brothers*, Pamela G. Wilson looks at the issue from the perspective of Black Christians, but what she says applies equally to people of all races and religions in America. "Too many Black Christians today continue to maintain alliances based on race, mostly because of the legacy of racial injustice in this country. As a result, Blacks have evolved into a monolithic machine; whose members learn by rote a 'Black viewpoint' that varies only slightly by social class. The dictionary defines this race-focused perspective as 'racialism' and those who practice it, 'racialists.'"[10]

Many who voted for President Obama were centrists who hoped he would help America take a major step forward in the area of race relations. These independent voters may not have accepted or even approved of candidate Obama's political platform, but for the prospect of better race relations they were willing to put their concerns aside and vote for the man they thought might close the racial gap. To these voters, Obama's handling of the Cambridge police incident represented a broken promise. Americans who thought they were voting for a racial healer were bitterly disappointed to see his knee-jerk racialist response to the confrontation between Cambridge police officers and Professor Gates. Further, the President's beer-in-the-Rose-Garden substitute for a sincere apology did little to allay their disappointment. The three parties involved met, had a beer at the White House, and went about their business, agreeing only to disagree. This episode is a textbook example of how not to build trust as a leader.

Trust and the Young Obama's Relationship with Frank Marshall Davis

In his book, *Dreams from My Father*, Barack Obama discusses his relationship with a friend of his grandfather's that he refers to only as "Frank." When candidate Obama was forced by events to admit that the mysterious Frank was actually Frank Marshall Davis, many Americans became concerned about how much influence Davis might have had on Obama during his formative years. The controversy surrounding the identity of Frank began when Gerald Horne wrote an article for *Political Affairs* in which he claimed that Frank was, in fact, Frank Marshall Davis and that Davis had been a "decisive influence" in the formation of Barack Obama's worldview.[11]

Frank Marshall Davis' connections to the Communist Party USA, connections that were investigated by the House Un-American Activities Committee (HUAC) in 1950, gave rise to speculation that he tutored young Obama in the ways of communism. This claim was explored in greater depth in Jerome Corsi's book, *The Obama Nation.* In this book, released during the presidential campaign, Corsi claimed that Davis strongly influenced the young Obama's political views.[12]

Candidate Obama claimed that Davis was just a friend of his grandfather's who had no effect on his political views. His campaign even released a book entitled *Unfit for Publication* attacking Corsi's claims and asserting that Davis was just a family friend, not a political mentor. The issue gained insufficient traction to derail Obama's bid for the presidency, but it did create yet another question that has undermined the President's ability to win the trust of all Americans. Further, as more and more details are revealed about Obama's socialistic approach to America's economic woes—in rhetoric and in policy the specter of Frank Marshall Davis continues to hover around the President like an apparition.

Trust and Obama's Promise of Post-Partisanship

President Obama's administration is turning out to be one of the most partisan in our nation's history. Partisan presidents are nothing new, but one of President Obama's campaign promises was that he would reverse this trend. One of the phrases heard often during Obama's campaign was about the "post-partisan future" he would achieve for America. He promised to move the country beyond the divisiveness of red and blue states and establish a sense of "unity of purpose."[13] But according to *Wall Street Journal* columnist, William McGurn:

> Six months into the president's term, you don't read much about this post-partisan future anymore. It may be because on almost every big-ticket legislative item (the stimulus, climate change, and now health care), Mr. Obama

has been pushing a highly ideological agenda with little (and in some cases zero) support from across the aisle. Yet far from stating the obvious—that sitting in the Oval Office is a very partisan president—the press corps is allowing Mr. Obama to evade the issue by coming up with novel redefinitions.[14]

Redefining what the concept of non-partisanship means, even with the assistance and support of the press, will not build trust for the President. This approach, now so characteristic of Obama, is nothing more than political spin and clever obfuscation. Americans know what non-partisanship means, and they know it is not happening. Rather, President Obama is using his majority in Congress to force through an agenda that many Americans find abhorrent and in the process is undermining further the trust of the people to whom he will eventually answer.

Trust and the Visitor Records Issue

Earlier in this chapter we explained that the watchdog group, Citizens for Responsibility and Ethics in Washington (CREW), had asked the Obama administration to release the visitation logs showing which healthcare and insurance executives had visited the White House. The clear implication of the request was that while he promised to hold all healthcare debates in public on C-SPAN, President Obama was actually conducting private meetings behind closed doors in the White House. The Obama administration not only refused to release the visitor logs, as is required by the Freedom of Information Act (FOIA), but it used the same rationale it had criticized the Bush administration for using in a similar situation.

Many Americans saw this as blatant hypocrisy. According

to Kara Rowland, columnist for the *Washington Times*:

> Mr. Obama and other Democrats repeatedly
> attacked Mr. Cheney for refusing to release
> records of private individuals who met with Mr.
> Cheney's energy task force early in the Bush
> administration. Mr. Cheney and others argued
> that the White house could not hold sensitive
> and confidential talks with top industry players
> in many cases if the meetings are made public.
> Now the White House is relying on many of the
> same arguments used by Mr. Cheney to prevent
> the release of industry executives meeting with
> the president and his aides on healthcare.[15]

Trust and Obama's Standing in Europe

President Obama's supporters are practically gleeful over
the results of a poll being called the *Global Attitude Poll* conducted by the Pew Research Center. This poll shows that since
the election of Barack Obama and the departure of George W.
Bush, America has shown double digit increases in popularity
among European nations. It is interesting and instructive that
the results of the *Global Attitude Poll* come at the same time
that the President's approval rating in his own country is plummeting.[16]

Unfortunately for the President, it appears that the joke is
on him. Being liked by Europeans is not an asset when many
Americans view European nations as nothing more than a
bunch of socialist countries in decline whose people have
over-inflated egos, short memories, and insufficient gratitude.
According to Senator John Danforth of Missouri, President
Obama's popularity in Europe has no value since it has not paid

off in any tangible way on difficult challenges such as the war in Afghanistan or in closing down the detention center at Guantanamo Bay, Cuba.[17] "I think the president is telling people what they want to hear. He's apologizing; he's saying we will get out of Iraq and close down Guantanamo. But when he does ask for something, he doesn't seem to get anything."[18]

There is an old maxim about knowing a person by his enemies. The obverse is also true: you can know a person by his friends. President Obama is scoring few points with Americans by being liked by the Europeans. Europeans like Barack Obama because he is philosophically one of them and is quick to apologize for America. But his supporters are confusing likability with respect. Everyone has known an individual they liked but did not respect. When it comes to international relations, it would be better for America if our allies and enemies respected President Obama. It would also be better if they knew without a doubt that he would stand firm for the best interests of the United States, regardless of whether that met with their approval or not. Whether our allies and enemies like the President does not matter, but whether they respect him does.

Trust and Obama's Handling of Foreign Affairs

Many Americans do not trust that President Obama has their best interests at heart when he interacts with foreign heads of state. The President of the United States wears several hats, all of them important. Arguably, the most important is foreign affairs. The occupant of the Oval Office is also the leader of the free world, which is what has many Americans concerned. Recent events in foreign affairs bode poorly for the United States and, in turn, the rest of the free world. In fact, they cause many Americans to question whether President Obama is up to the job of leading our country in the crucial area of foreign affairs.

Representing the United States in foreign affairs is like playing three-dimensional chess with an ever-changing set of rules. It is a complex game with the highest possible stakes that demands vision, courage, commitment, stealth, steely nerves, a willingness to take calculated risks, and a thorough understanding of the concept of national interest—ours as well as those of our enemies and allies. What it does not require is that our allies or enemies like the President. Being the leader of the free world is playing in the big leagues where everyone plays for keeps and there is little room for error. Observing President Obama's performance in foreign affairs so far causes many Americans to wonder if he is really up to the job.

Just a few examples of the President's performance in foreign affairs suggest he needed to spend more time in the minor league before jumping to the majors. His handling of the Guantanamo issue embarrassed his administration and party. His public statements on North Korea, although on target, are having little effect. Unlike the American public, North Korean officials are not swayed by speeches, no matter how well-delivered. After Obama labeled a nuclear-armed North Korea a "grave threat," the communist government thumbed its nose at the President by having two American journalists arrested and sentenced to 12 years of hard labor.

The Obama administration was able to eventually secure the release of the two women, but only after making groveling apologies to North Korea—something President Obama could certainly relate to and is quite good at. The journalists were returned to America, which is good. But Americans still do not know what President Obama gave up to secure their release, which is not good. In the meantime, North Korea continues to develop nuclear weapons undeterred by Obama's rhetoric. There is a lesson in this if the President is paying attention.

Perhaps Obama's biggest foreign-affairs blunder thus far was his reluctant response to election fraud in Iran and to the bigger issue of nuclear proliferation in a country that is the poster child for the "hate-America" movement. To date, Obama's attempts to reason with the anti-American government of this rogue nation have met with predictable results. Obama administration rhetoric has changed from that of previous administrations on Iran's nuclear capability. Whereas previous administrations made it clear that Iran would not be allowed to deploy nuclear weapons, the Obama administration has quietly changed the message to "when" Iran deploys nuclear weapons.

Words alone are not sufficient when the stability of the world depends in large measure on America's strength and resolve. Teddy Roosevelt knew this when he said, "Walk softly and carry a big stick." His big stick was America's great white fleet of battleships. He put the fleet on display in a worldwide voyage to send a message to our allies and enemies about American strength and resolve. President Reagan followed suit when he said, "Mr. Gorbachev, tear down this wall." Then to back up this courageous statement, he threatened to deploy the Strategic Defense Initiative (SDI). Journalists in America scoffed at the idea, calling it "Star Wars." But the Soviet Union didn't scoff, and the rest is history. In the meantime, President Obama is cutting military spending as a way to help fund his socialistic energy, economic, and healthcare initiatives.

Contrast the boldness, clarity, and resolve of Presidents Roosevelt and Reagan with the tentative, tepid actions of President Obama and what comes to mind is a latter-day version of Jimmy Carter, albeit a more articulate version. Even his detractors admit that President Obama is an articulate speaker. If his teleprompter doesn't break, he can deliver a moving speech. Unfortunately, the world leaders he must deal with are not like

American voters—they don't confuse image with substance. Rather, they have the self-interested instincts of a shark for detecting vulnerability. If Obama appears weak or naive, our allies will lose faith in America and make the best deal they can with our enemies. In the meantime, our enemies will do what sharks always do—circle their prey and look for opportunities to attack.

Trust and Obama's Naiveté in Foreign Policy

In the previous section, we explained the potentially disastrous effects of the President of the United States being naive in foreign affairs. Unfortunately, President Obama's actions to date make him appear to be precisely that—naive. This fact undermines the trust Americans should have in their president. To date, Barack Obama's success in politics has been based primarily on talk. He talked his way into the Illinois state legislature, talked his way into the United States Senate, and talked his way into the Oval Office. One thing is certain about this president—he is a talker. He comes across well on television, at least to an electorate conditioned to focus on image rather than substance. In fact, talking has worked so well for the President in his political career that we can understand—but not excuse—his thinking it will work equally well on the international stage. It won't.

President Obama's approach to foreign policy is based on a willingness to talk to any world leader who, in his words, will "unclench" his fist. So far this approach has been well-received by the political left who, like the President, believe that everyone in the world thinks like they do. But what Obama does not seem to understand is that the despots of the world he is so willing to talk with are not at all like this. Our enemies will unclench their fists alright, but just long enough to grasp a dagger to stab our naive President in the back. Nor does Obama seem to appreciate that giving an audience to these despots will serve to legitimize some of the most disreputable tyrants since Hitler and Stalin.

By far, the most serious problem with the President's *talk-with-anyone* approach to foreign policy is that while he talks, our enemies act. To Obama, talking is a way to persuade others to accept his point of view. But to the leaders of North Korea, Iran, and other rogue nations bent on America's destruction, talk is only a tactic used to buy the time needed to gain geopolitical advantage. Because of his naiveté, President Obama is ignoring one of the most fundamental rules of foreign policy: know your enemy. One need go back in history no further than 1968 to see what happens when this rule is ignored. Lyndon Johnson's presidency imploded because he failed to know his enemy—the North Vietnamese communists.

Johnson, like Obama, was a talker—albeit a behind-the-scenes kind. He thought he could apply his old Senatorial negotiating philosophy of "come and let's reason together" to North Vietnamese communists. While Johnson's negotiators spent months talking to smiling communist diplomats in Paris, the North Vietnamese Army used the time to maneuver for advantage. The longer they talked in Paris, the greater the military advantage gained by the communists. And, of course, the ink was hardly dry on the Paris Peace Treaty before the communist leaders simply ignored it and pressed their military advantage. Then came the killing fields, the "re-education" camps, and the displacement of tens of thousands of South Vietnamese refugees.

If Obama would spend less time reading from a teleprompter and more time reading from a history book, he could learn from Johnson's mistake. But this is not likely to happen. Like most glib talkers, the President is a one-trick pony. Ask a barber to solve a problem and he will give you a haircut. Ask a talker to solve a problem and he will give you talk. Unwilling to learn the lessons of history, the President naively pursues his verbal diplomacy and, as a result, the world becomes more dangerous for Americans every day.

The Koreans, Iranians, and other rogue nations know our history better than we do, and in Obama they see another Johnson, someone they can stall with talk while maneuvering for advantage. This is precisely what is happening. The Russians—themselves masters of stall-by-talking diplomacy— also welcome so-called dialogue with Obama. Why wouldn't they? Even a foreign-policy novice can see that when it comes to Obama's presidency, time is on the side of those who want America to fall. The longer he talks, the weaker America's geo-political position becomes.

Perhaps where Obama's approach to foreign policy is most immediately dangerous is in dealing with the puppet President of Iran and the ayatollahs who pull his strings. President Ah madinejad and Iran's anti-American ayatollahs are skilled prac-titioners of a concept known as *taqiyya*. This is a Muslim term that in essence means tactical hypocrisy. In plain terms, the Quran not only allows Muslims to lie, deceive, and obfuscate when it serves their purposes, it encourages the practice.

In spite of the voter fraud debacle and the on-going deaths of Iranian dissidents that began to occur in July of 2009, Presi-dent Obama is still working through back channels to arrange talks with key leaders in Iran. At some point, Ayatollah Ali Khamenei might order Ahmadinejad to unclench his fist long enough to hold talks with President Obama. If this happens, let's hope the President will be on guard against Ahmadine-jad's other fist; the one clenching the dagger he will plunge into America's back.

Trust and Obama's Historical Revisionism

According to President Obama, America is not a Christian nation. When more than 70 percent of Americans claim to be Christians, is it any wonder that so many do not trust the President? Obama first made this absurd claim while serving in the U.S. Senate. He made it again while campaigning for the presidency. More recently, he repeated his assertion while on a trip to Turkey. It is not our purpose in this book to provide the remedial instruction in U.S. history our President so obviously needs. This has already been done in two well-written and comprehensively-documented articles—one by Gary De-Mar[19] and another by David Barton.[20] We can add nothing to the work of these scholars here. Rather, we will offer two comments that are pertinent.

First, America is a Christian nation because it was founded by Christian men and women seeking religious liberty, established according to Christian principles, and shaped by Christian values. Second, remedial instruction would not help the President because his denials of our country's Christian heritage are based on politics, not ignorance—a fact that makes him all the more culpable.

Our purpose is to show that in claiming that America is not a Christian nation, Obama is engaging in an underhanded practice that is not worthy of a President of the United States and will certainly not build trust. The practice we reference is known as *historical revisionism*. Historical revisionism is the intentional distortion of the factual record for the purpose of advancing a specific agenda—in Obama's case a left-wing political agenda. The *modus operandi* of the historical revisionist is to distort the truth and then repeat the distortion until there is no longer any debate about it in the minds of the audience—in this case the American public.

Historical revisionism is intellectual dishonesty at its worst. Its practitioners are often highly-educated people—Obama graduated *magna cum laude* from Harvard Law School—who use their intellectual skills to cynically manipulate an audience they assume to be ill-informed and easily swayed. They do this by deliberately distorting history using such tactics as ignoring evidence that runs counter to their political agenda, twisting facts to support their presuppositions, and obfuscating when their opinions are challenged. Unfortunately, Obama appears to know his audience well—at least when it comes to American history. Few peoples of the world are so ignorant of their own history as Americans. When it comes to the history of our nation, Americans are easy prey for historical revisionists—especially one who speaks with the authority of the President of the United States and is aided and abetted by a liberal press.

In stooping to the practice of historical revisionism, President Obama has joined a smarmy band of brothers. His fellow revisionists are responsible for some of the most infamous distortions of history ever perpetrated. Just a few examples of these distortions include: 1) denial that the Holocaust, in which more than six million Jews were exterminated, ever happened, 2) characterizing Mao's "Great Leap Forward" in which more than 40 million Chinese starved to death as a salutary event in the history of China, and 3) claiming that Japanese atrocities during World War II—such as forcing women into sexual slavery—are a myth. We do not claim that President Obama believes these great lies, but that he is knowingly advancing what, like these lies, is an easily refutable myth.

Now add to these nonsensical distortions Obama's claim that America is not a Christian nation and the deceitful nature of historical revisionism becomes clear. What makes Obama's revisionist claims even worse than those of his fellow distorters is the seat he occupies. No president who denies the history of the country he is sworn to protect, defend, and lead is worthy of the office.

President Obama has turned out to be one of those people you trust less and less as you get to know him more and more. In some cases, even those who supported his candidacy and voted for him are becoming concerned about his trustworthiness. In numerous cases, he said one thing during the presidential campaign and did another as President. He made promises and broke them. When questioned about the differences between his promises and his actions, he has waffled, equivocated, obfuscated, and—many believe—outright lied. The honeymoon is over and the historical significance of being America's first African-American president is no longer enough to convince the public to give him a pass. The more that Americans learn about the details of his policies—both foreign and domestic—the further President Obama's approval rating will fall. Much of the reason for this decline is that a growing number of Americans do not believe they can trust their president.

NOTES

1. Stewart J. Black and Hall B. Gregersen, *Leading Strategic Change: Breaking Through the Brain Barrier* (Upper Saddle River, NJ: Prentice Hall Financial Times, 2002), 16.

2. WorldNet Daily. "AOL poll: 82% want Obama to release it." Retrieved from http://www.wnd.com/index.php?fa=PAGE. view&pageId=105023 on July 25, 2009.

3. Alex Koppelman, "Obama dodges question on his transparency promises," *WAR ROOM*, Wednesday, July 22, 2009. Retrieved from http://salon.com/politics/war_room/2009/07/22/obama_ transparency/ on July 29, 2009.

4. Ibid.

5. As quoted in "You Can't Trust Obama. Trust Us." Retrieved from http://swampland.blogs.time.com/2008/09/18/you_cant_trust_obama_trust_us/ on July 29, 2009.

6. Thomas Sowell, "A post-racial president?" Retrieved from www.onenewsnow.com/Perspectives/Default.aspx?id=621886 on July 30, 2009.

7. Ibid.

8. Ibid.

9. Ibid.

10. Pamela G. Wilson, *Finding Soul Brothers: Dismantling Black Christian Racialism,* (Bloomington, IN: AuthorHouse, 2007), front cover flap.

11. Gerald Horne, "Rethinking the History and Future of the Communist Party, *Political Affairs Magazine,* March 28, 2007.

12. Jerome Corsi, *The Obama Nation* (New York, NY: Simon and Schuster, 2008), 85.

13. Greg Pierce (compiler), "Inside Politics," *Washington Times,* July 27, 2009, 14.

14. William McGurn, As quoted in "Inside Politics" compiled by Greg Pierce, *Washington Times,* July 27, 2009, 14.

15. Kara Rowland, "Obama hold on visitor records raises cries of hypocrisy," *Washington Times,* July 27, 2009, 3.

16. Joe Curl, "Albright: Obama's made us cool again," *Washington Times,* July 27, 2009, 11.

17. Ibid.

18. As quoted in "Albright: Obama's made us cool again," by Joe Curl, *Washington Times,* July 11, 2009, 11.

19. Gary DeMar, "Were the Founders Diests?" Retrieved from http://www.americanvision.org/the-american-vision-blog/were-the-founders-deists/ on July 8, 2009.

20. David Barton, "Is President Obama Correct: Is America No

Longer a Christian Nation?" Retrieved from http://wallbuilders. com/LIBissuesArticles.asp?id=23909 on July 8, 2009.

FOUR

Why Does President Obama Lack Credibility?

"The pastor of my church, Reverend Jeremiah
Wright,... has touched off a firestorm over the
last few days. He's drawn attention as the result
of some inflammatory and appalling remarks he
made about our country, our politics, and my
political opponents."

—Barack Obama
As quoted in *The Huffington Post*

Credibility is what a leader has when the people he is supposed to lead believe in him, can relate to him, know he has their best interests at heart, and are confident that he knows what he is doing. In other words, credibility is like trust in that a leader must gain it, build on it, and maintain it. Also like trust, credibility is hard to earn but easy to lose. This fact bodes poorly for President Obama. The better Americans get to know him and his associates, the less inclined they are to believe in him, think they can relate to him, feel sure he has their best interests at heart, and view him as competent in his position as president.

The controversy that exploded around him during the presidential campaign concerning his long and close relationship with Reverend Jeremiah Wright is just the tip of the iceberg in terms of why President Obama lacks credibility with so many Americans. The fact that he quickly disassociated himself from

Reverend Wright when the twenty-year relationship threatened to submarine his presidential campaign, rather than adding to his credibility, just undermined it even further. Obama's handling of the Reverend Wright affair made him appear as a political opportunist who would say anything, deny anything, and do anything to be president—not a way to build credibility. The Reverend Wright affair is examined later in this chapter.

In addition to the Reverend Wright fiasco, this chapter explores several other issues that tend to undermine President Obama's credibility with a substantial cross-section of American citizens. The issues fall into the two categories of religion and respect for the military. Each of these categories carries within it an informal, unstated test that American presidents must pass if they are to have credibility with the majority of the American public. To put a fine point on it, Americans want to know, without question or equivocation, where their president stands on God and the military. They want to know without a doubt that he respects God and the military and places a sufficiently high priority on them.

Further, Americans tend to hold the President responsible for the attitudes of his supporters toward God and the military. Try as he might, Obama cannot effectively distance himself from the Reverend Wright's inflammatory diatribes, nor can he distance himself from the anti-God and anti-military views of his most reliable base of support—the far left.

It is not enough for the President to voice tepid support for God and the military when his most ardent supporters seem bent on tearing them down. Americans expect the President's attitude toward God and the military to be positive and they expect his actions to match his words. Further, they expect him to play a leadership role in making sure that support for God and the military does not wane on his watch.

The fact that just the opposite is happening during his administration is undermining President Obama's credibility with many Americans.

Obama, His Supporters, and Religion in America

Even taking into account Reverend Wright's anti-American diatribes—words that Obama disingenuously claims he never heard during twenty years of attending Wright's church—many Americans are more concerned by the fact that Obama's most ardent supporters are secular humanists. When these Obama supporters use the terms "Christian" or "Christian Right," more often than not they intend them to be pejoratives; this is blatant arrogance in a country where more than 70 percent of citizens identify themselves as Christians. The secular humanistic attitudes, practices, and policies of the Obama administration and his strongest supporters are undermining the President's credibility.

Freedom FROM religion is a fundamental tenet of secular humanism. The Left's interpretation of the First Amendment is that it requires a forced segregation of religion from all aspects of public life. This is both a disingenuous and hypocritical interpretation. The disingenuous aspect is that the Left knowingly and purposefully misinterprets the "Establishment" and "Free Exercise" clauses of the First Amendment which say: "Congress shall make no law respecting an establishment of religion, or prohibiting the free exercise thereof..." Beyond choosing to ignore the historical fact that our founders intended this language to protect against the type of state-supported established church they had fled England to avoid, their interpretation is disingenuous because it focuses solely on the first clause while completely ignoring the second.

The hypocritical aspect of the Left's interpretation of the First Amendment is that they are not really opposed to religion *per se*, just the Christian religion—a fact that is hurting President Obama by association. The President has compounded his problems in this critical area by avoiding Christian symbols in his public appearances and supporting such legislation as the "hate crime" bill. Obama's supporters typically bend over backwards to accommodate Islam, Hinduism, and Buddhism. For example, President Obama's comment made during a foreign junket about the United States being one of the largest Muslim countries in the world was little more than a fabrication made to pander to his Muslim audience (America's Muslim population would rank it as 38th in the world).

Obama's supporters on the Left are just as religious as Christians; the difference is found in whom and what they worship. While Christians worship the omniscient, never-changing Creator and Ruler of the universe, secular humanists worship a limited and ever-changing god—man. The religion of the Left is secular humanism and it is practiced with all the passion of the most zealous Christians of any denomination.

Because, as Christians, God is our authority, we believe in right and wrong and look to the Bible for guidance in distinguishing between the two. God's specific revelation concerning who He is, who we are, and how we should live is found in Holy Scripture. Hence, regardless of denomination, the Bible provides a common starting point for helping Christians make determinations about right and wrong.

Putting aside for the moment the fact that God is the ultimate authority concerning right and wrong, whether those on the Left wish to admit it or not, it is important to have a common starting point when discussing and debating such matters. Consider what happens when two people try to settle an issue of right and wrong, but lack a common basis for deciding. They are like two surveyors trying to settle a property dispute who begin their work from two different points of reference. The claim will never be settled. The only way one survey can either validate or refute another is if the surveyors started at a common point of reference. The lesson in this analogy is one that secular humanists choose to ignore. Those who do not wish to be bound by the moral constraints of Christianity must find an alternative. That alternative, at least for the Left, is secular humanism. While Christians look to the Bible and the example of Christ for guidance in matters of right and wrong, secular humanists rely on the concept of moral relativism. Moral relativism is the concept that underlies such bedrock policies of the left as abortion on demand and homosexual marriage—both of which have President Obama's enthusiastic support.

Moral Relativism Defined

Moral relativism is a fundamental tenet of the secular humanist's worldview. It claims right and wrong are culturally-based and man-made, thus they are subject to the determination of the individual. If God decides right and wrong and man is god, then man decides right and wrong. In layman's terms, moral relativism means that there are no absolutes; each individual can decide for himself what is right and what is wrong and act accordingly.

Secular humanists believe in the evolutionary view that life on earth is the result of random cosmic accidents. This being the case, life is accidental and therefore lacks any meaning. Consequently, anything the individual chooses to do is acceptable because in the long run it is not going to matter anyway. From the convenient perspective of moral relativism, if something is right for me, it is right period; an attractive point of view for those who feel constrained by the Judeo-Christian ethic. In adopting moral relativism as part of their worldview, secular humanists are applying a strategy that is as old as mankind itself: if the rules get in the way of what you want, make new rules. The Obama administration, with the help of Congress, is working hard to change the rules that many Americans believe are essential to the well-being of a civilized society.

Is Moral Relativism Really Morally Neutral?

Secular humanists like to claim that moral relativism—you do your thing and I'll do mine—is a morally neutral concept. This misguided attitude has had a devastating effect on policies coming out of Washington, D.C. In the first place, the concept of moral neutrality is a practical impossibility—nothing is morally neutral. In an article entitled, "Moral Relativism – Neutral Thinking," the president of Planned Parenthood is quoted as saying, "teaching morality doesn't mean imposing my moral values on others. It means sharing wisdom, giving reasons for believing as I do—and then trusting others to think and judge for themselves."[1] Even a cursory reading of this statement reveals the absurdity of the claim. The only reason for making such a statement is to influence the thinking of others. If moral relativism were a valid concept, there would be no reason to try to influence others. Hence, the arguments for moral relativism are, by their very nature, self-refuting.

Secular humanists who argue for moral relativism argue against themselves. For example, tell a proponent of moral relativism that you advocate child abuse and you are likely to be reported to government authorities. However, if the secular humanist who reports you really believes that right and wrong are matters of individual choice, how can he argue against child abuse? After all, there are certainly individuals—many of them—who choose to abuse children. Let the reader understand that we use this example only to illustrate the absurdity of moral relativism—we are not in any way condoning or endorsing child abuse. What the moral relativist really believes is that what is right is what he thinks is right at any given moment in time.

Because of the inherent flaw in their philosophy, secular humanists have taken to adding a disclaimer to their arguments for moral relativism. They now say that whatever the individual believes is right unless it hurts someone else. But, of course, the disclaimer is as flawed as the concept. If everything is relative, it cannot be wrong to hurt someone else. If it is wrong to hurt someone else, why do moral relativists support abortion, a heinous act that hurts the unborn child, the mother, and society? There is no end to these types of questions, and no acceptable answer to them from proponents of moral relativism. Logic is not on the side of secular humanists, nor is credibility.

Obviously, moral relativism is a flawed concept. None the less, it is considered sacred ground among members of the Left. For example, colleges and universities are virtual breeding grounds for the concept of moral relativism. A Zogby poll shows that 75 percent of college professors teach that there is no such thing as right and wrong—that good and evil are relative concepts based on individual and cultural interpretation.[2] Yet, these same professors are quick to claim that Christian and conservative worldviews are wrong, a fact that undermines the credibility of the Left and President Obama.

Consider what Robert Brandon, professor of biology and philosophy at Duke University, had to say when questioned about liberal bias at his institution: "If, as John Stuart Mill said, stupid people are generally conservative, then there are lots of conservatives we will never hire... Members of academia tend to be a bit smarter than average."[3]   This is an example of the arrogance now associated with the Obama administration and his supporters.

William McGuffey, author of the classic elementary school readers used to teach generations of Americans, said: "Erase all thought and fear of God from a community, and selfishness and sensuality will absorb the whole man."[4]   This is a prophetic statement because it provides an accurate description of what is happening in America as a byproduct of the teaching of secular humanism and its subset, moral relativism.

Humanist Manifesto:
The Bible for Humanists/Moral Relativists

Like many religions, secular humanism has a "bible," a sacred text from which it derives its doctrines. Liberals look to the *Humanist Manifesto* as their sacred book. There are actually three versions of the *Manifesto*: 1) the original *Humanist Manifesto* published in 1933 (*Humanist Manifesto* I), 2) *Humanist Manifesto* II published in 1973, and 3) *Humanism and Its Aspirations* published in 2003 (*Humanist Manifesto* III). All three of these documents describe a worldview absent of God or any other kind of higher power. The God of humanism is man. All three versions of the *Manifesto* have been signed by prominent members of the Left.

The *Manifesto* has been updated and revised over time as humanist thinking has ebbed and flowed and as disagreements among its proponents have emerged. The fickle nature of man is just one of many factors that undermines the fundamental validity of a man-centered religion. Consequently, each successive version of the *Manifesto* has sought to correct the perceived weaknesses of its predecessor and rebut criticisms from both the Right and Left.

Humanist Manifesto I

The original *Manifesto,* written in 1933, presented a new belief system to replace religions founded on supernatural revelation. The new belief system it proposed amounted to an egalitarian worldview based on voluntary mutual cooperation among all people; an ideal rendered impossible from the outset in the real world by the sinful nature of man. Predictably, there was disagreement about various aspects of the *Manifesto* among those involved in developing it, a circumstance inherent in all human endeavors. Consequently, the originally proposed title, "*The Humanist Manifesto,*" had to be changed to "*A Humanist Manifesto.*"

Ironically, the original *Manifesto* contained a basic tenet that now haunts, embarrasses, and even angers the Left today. It referred to humanism as a religion, something the Left goes to great lengths to deny since freedom FROM religion is the cornerstone of their man-centered worldview, as well as a rhetorical strategy by which to replace Christianity with their own religion and agenda. If secular humanists admit that their views of morality are a religion, the hypocrisy of their efforts to ban religion from the classroom, public square, and marketplace of ideas is exposed. If this happens, the Left will be forced to admit that Christianity is their real target, not religion. This, of course, is something that even a casual observer of the American culture wars already knows from the Left's rhetorical, literary, and artistic attacks on Christianity and its pseudo-legal war on public and private expressions of the Christian faith.

Humanist Manifesto II

The horrors of World War II perpetrated by the followers of Hitler and Stalin in Europe, not to mention those of Tojo in China, exploded the ideal at the heart of the original *Mani-*

festo. With the evidence of Hitler's death camps, Stalin's po-
groms, and Tojo's rape of Nanking revealed to the world, even
the most idealistic of humanists had to admit that their hope
for a worldwide egalitarian society based on voluntary mutual
cooperation might have been a little too optimistic. One can
only wonder why the horrors of World War II did not lead humanists to abandon the concept of moral relativism, for if the
concept were valid there would be nothing morally wrong with
any of these horrific actions.

Admitting the naiveté of the first document, drafters of
the revised *Manifesto* took a more expedient approach. Rather
than pursuing a worldwide egalitarian society based on voluntary mutual cooperation, the drafters of *Manifesto* II set more
"realistic" goals, including the elimination of war and poverty.
Of course, if intellectual and moral relativism were valid concepts, there would be nothing wrong with war and no reason to
eliminate poverty. Naturally, this logical thought did not occur to the learned authors of the *Manifesto*, and none of the
document's supporters thought to ask how these goals could be
achieved without changing the heart of man.

Such it is and has always been with the Left. Since man is god,
why try to change his heart? Simply coerce his behavior through
intrusive government policies and prescriptive laws. When one
will not admit that man has a sinful nature, it is easy to naively
think that war and hunger can be eliminated by displaying heart-
tugging bumper stickers on your car, a favorite tactic of the Left.
After all, slogans such as "Give Peace a Chance"—if displayed on
enough bumpers—will end war, won't they?

One of the most controversial and frequently quoted vers-
es from *Manifesto* II is: "We are responsible for what we are
and what we will be... No deity will save us; we must save ourselves."[5] How does the Left propose to save mankind? The an-

swer to this question is what scares so many Americans and undermines President Obama's credibility: through government programs. Another verse, one that clearly reveals a cherished goal of the Left is:

> The battleground for humankind's future must be waged and won in the public school classroom by teachers who correctly perceive their role as the proselytizers of a new faith: a religion of humanity that recognizes and respects the spark of what theologians call divinity in every human being... Utilizing a classroom instead of a pulpit to convey humanist values in whatever subject they teach, regardless of the educational level—preschool day care or large state university.[6]

Professions of the Left's faith such as this scare many Americans who are concerned about the indoctrination of their children. Because of such admissions, many Americans have come to believe that President Obama and the Left want to insert themselves between parents and their children.

As is always the case in the endeavors of man, there was much disagreement in the liberal community about various aspects of *Manifesto* II. Consequently, only a few ardent proponents agreed to sign the document when it was first released. To solve this problem, the *Manifesto* has since been widely circulated with a caveat making it clear that it is not necessary to agree with every detail of the document in order to be a signatory. This disclaimer had the intended effect, and the document eventually garnered more signatures.

Humanist Manifesto III

The latest version of the *Manifesto—Humanist Manifesto III*—is titled, *Humanism and Its Aspirations.* It was published by the American Humanist Association in 2003. This version of the *Manifesto* is purposefully shorter than its predecessors. It presents six broad beliefs that encompass the humanist philosophy as professed by the American Humanist Association, but that leave plenty of room for interpretation, this latter characteristic being necessary to avoid much of the disagreement within humanist circles that surrounded the two early versions of the *Manifesto.* These six broad statements of belief may be summarized as follows:

- Knowledge of the world is empirically derived (by observation, experimentation, and rational analysis).

- Unguided evolutionary change has the result of making humans integral to nature.

- Ethical values are established by humans and are based on human need that has been tested by experience.

- Humans are fulfilled in life by participating in the service of humane ideals.

- Humans are, by nature, social beings. Therefore, they find meaning in relationships.

- Humans maximize their happiness by working to benefit society. [7]

Although these six statements of belief are not as specific as those contained in the early versions of the *Manifesto*, they still support the same worldview. For example, the first statement—

the humanist belief in empiricism—rules out God's special revelation as set forth in the Bible and reveals an astounding ignorance of the philosophical problems inherent in man-centered empiricism. The second statement is a reiteration of the humanist belief in Darwinian evolution which, of course, is the American Humanist Association's knock on creationism, as well as its justification for supporting abortion, a bedrock plank in the platform of Obama's most reliable supporters.

The third statement makes clear that the Bible has no place in establishing right and wrong. Rather, what is right or wrong depends on human need and human experience. The statement conveniently overlooks the anti-ethical implications of irrational, chance-based evolutionism; the futility of attempting to deduce right and wrong from human needs; and the impossibility of deciding by what standard to evaluate human experience in a meaningless evolutionary world. The last three statements make clear the humanist's rejection of God, the Bible, and religion. In the fourth statement, fulfillment comes from the service of humane ideals, not service to God and His Kingdom. Why this is so in a morally relativistic world is not explained.

Christians also believe in service, but they know that service to man comes from Christ's admonition to love your neighbor as yourself. In the fifth statement, human relationships are presented as the ultimate goal, as opposed to a relationship with God. How humans can find such meaning in a meaningless evolutionary world is not explained. Finally, humanists believe that service to society is the ultimate service because, for them, man is god. Christians also believe in service to society, but as a way to serve the God who created man and to follow Christ's admonition to love our neighbors as ourselves. Christians have a solid philosophical foundation for their belief in service to society.   Secular humanism's faith in irrational evolutionary change and empiricism, however, cannot provide an adequate philosophical foundation for serving humane ideals, finding meaning in relationships, or maximizing happiness by working to benefit society.

Manifesto III is shorter and more to the point than its predecessors, and its six statements of belief are less specific, but its rejection of God is just as much a cornerstone as it was in the early versions. The wording and length of the various versions of the *Manifesto* have changed over time, but its foundational man-as-god philosophy has not.   Herein is found the never-changing source of the unbridgeable gulf between secular humanism and Christianity.   Herein also is found the source of the Left's religious bigotry toward Christianity, a bigotry that undermines President Obama's credibility with a substantial number of Americans.

Secular humanists apparently believe they can peacefully co-exist with other religions—hence their accommodation of Islam, Hinduism, and Buddhism.   In fact, they tolerate all worldviews except one: Christianity.   Although there is a philosophical and practical train wreck coming farther down the track involving secular humanists and Islam, for now the Left has focused its animosity on Christianity, because they know that if Christianity is right, they are wrong.   They also know, but refuse to admit, that Christianity is the foundation of western civilization. This simple fact frightens secular humanists so much that they feel compelled to belittle, attack, and even suppress the Christian worldview wherever and whenever it dares to rear its head.

Secular Humanism's Rationale for Moral Relativism

Since their god is man, it was necessary for secular humanists to establish an ethical corollary to humanism that would
render black and white standards of right and wrong obso-
lete. "During much of early American history, moral education in colleges and universities moved from being grounded
in appeals to special revelation to universal appeals to human
nature, natural law, or reason. In other words, teachers and
textbook writers attempted to locate moral agreement in something common to all humanity."[8] Thus was born the concept
of moral relativism. Of course, a fundamental flaw that its proponents have never been able to adequately explain is that the
only things common to all of humanity are its creation by God
and its sinful nature, neither of which secular humanists can
admit to. Nevertheless, when your god is man with all of his
inherent moral frailties, moral relativism is the best you can do
in the way of an ethical framework.

In order for secular humanism to prevail in American society, it is necessary for its proponents to control—or at least
influence—the institutions that together weave the tapestry of
its moral and social values. This is why the Left is so intent on
dominating institutions of higher education, and of education
in general. Anne Colby, writing for the *Journal of College and
Character,* had this to say about why the domination of colleges
and universities is so important to the Left:

> Many kinds of social institutions have
> important roles to play in educating citizens.
> Religious organizations and other voluntary
> associations, the media, and education at the
> elementary and secondary levels are among the
> most important of these. But higher education
> is critical, because universities and colleges

are the institutions most clearly charged with leading the development of new and deeper understanding through research and scholarship and preparing new generations by teaching not only information and skills, but their significance for creating the future, both personally and collectively. Higher education has tremendous opportunities for being a positive force in society as it reaches an ever larger segment of the population, including virtually all leaders in both government and the private sector. It is a powerful influence in shaping individual's relationships with each other and their communities, and we need to take steps to ensure its influence is constructive rather than corrosive.[9]

This statement provides irrefutable evidence of the Left's need to suppress the moral absolutes of Christianity and replace them with the ever-changing whims of moral relativism, evidence which is certainly corroborated by the Left's action in America's colleges and universities.

Values-Neutrality and Christianity

One of the arguments frequently heard from moral relativists to justify suppressing biblical views in the public square is that society should be values-neutral, an absurd argument made to appeal to the naive. Those who make this argument claim that values should be addressed by the family and church, but strictly omitted in all public endeavors and institutions. While Christians will certainly agree that families and churches should play the key role in establishing values in individuals, there are several problems with this argument. The most fundamental of these problems is that it represents a practical impossibility. Even if teachers, professors, elected officials, and government bureaucrats tried to be values-neutral, they could not possibly achieve such a goal. Everyone has a worldview that is based on specific values and those values govern the decisions they make, attitudes they adopt, viewpoints they espouse, and things they do. Another problem with the argument is the hypocrisy in it. The Left, President Obama's most dependable support base, invests much time and effort in trying to undermine the values they claim should be left to the development of families and churches.

One of the ways the Left attempts to undermine Christian and conservative worldviews is by turning educational institutions into leftist indoctrination centers. According to Colby, "closer scrutiny makes it clear that educational institutions cannot be values neutral. For decades educators have recognized the power of the 'hidden curriculum' in schools and the moral messages it carries. The hidden curriculum is the (largely unexamined) practices through which the school and its teachers operate, maintaining discipline, assigning grades and other rewards, and managing their relationships with their students and each other."[10]   She continues, "most of life's situations are inherently ambiguous, and their moral significance is underdetermined by available facts. In order to find meaning and clarity amid this ambiguity, people develop habits of moral interpretation and intuition through which they perceive the world."[11]

Members of the Left understand that "people develop habits of moral interpretation and intuition through which they perceive the world." They want to control the development. This is why they are so determined to supplant the Christian worldview with one that embraces moral relativism. People who conduct their lives according to the presuppositions of secular humanism, but maintain adversarial relationships with Christians and conservatives, are being anything but values-neutral. Further, secular humanists do not really want anyone else to be values-neutral. Rather, they want everyone else in the world to put aside their own values and embrace those of the Left. The reader should note that there are, of course, right-wing secular humanists (*e.g.* secular libertarians). However, our focus is on the overwhelmingly mainstream of modern secularism, which is left-wing and collectivist.

Society's Struggle with the Consequences of Moral Relativism

Secular humanists, with their devotion to moral relativism, are continually sticking their heads in an intellectual vise, one jaw of which is formed by their professed beliefs and the other by the consequences of those beliefs. Secular humanists cling tenaciously to the non-absolutes of moral relativism, while on the other hand deploring their consequences. Those consequences, when combined, can be summarized in two words: moral decay. Secular humanism has led to a high divorce rate, children born out of wedlock, fathers who abandon their families, drugs, rampant violence, abortion, a growing acceptance of homosexuality, and a general coarsening of American society.

If morality is relative and self-determined, then an immoral practice such as cheating is wrong only if one gets caught because honesty has value only to the extent it serves one's purpose at the moment. If morality is relative, then my only responsibility is to my own personal needs or desires at any given point in time. Further, people who proclaim tolerance as a fundamental aspect of their worldview do not practice tolerance when they treat Christian and conservative members of society intolerantly. When there is only one point of view allowed in a discussion, that is not tolerance. Society does not somehow become tolerant of diversity by being openly intolerant of it. These are the conundrums the Left inflicts on itself by advocating moral relativism while suppressing Christian and conservative views.

The Case Against Moral Relativism

To its proponents, one of the appealing aspects of moral relativism is that it precludes the need for discussion, debate, and disagreement. There are plenty of people who just want to be left alone to do their own thing and do not want to be bothered with discussions of right and wrong. Although these types of people are typically just as liberal as the more vocal members of the Left, they would rather let someone else fight the battles. Relativism allows these moral hermits to avoid conflict by simply adopting a *you-do-your-thing-and-I-will-do-mine* attitude toward the rest of the world.

Perhaps the most appealing aspect of moral relativism is that it allows proponents to get away with doing whatever they want. It is the perfect philosophy for people who do not wish to have their behavior constrained or their lifestyle inhibited by the rules. This aspect of moral relativism is why Ryan Dobson calls it "sin in a toga," by which he means that it is nothing more than "selfishness and hedonism and rebellion dressed up in philosopher's robes."[12] In his book, *Be Intolerant Because Some Things are Just Stupid,* Dobson says:

> Moral relativism is not a philosophy you would
> arrive at by studying the world around you. If
> you put something under your microscope or
> do real science with your chemistry set or point

your telescope at the stars, you will not arrive at
the conclusion that there are no constants in the
universe. The only way to come up with moral
relativism is to begin with an agenda and then
look for ways to make your agenda possible.
Your starting point is not an observation of the
universe, but an action you want to take.[13]

This is an important point because one of the foundational te-
nets of secular humanism is empiricism: the belief that knowledge of the world is gained through observation, experimentation, and rational analysis as opposed to biblical revelation.
Ironically, empiricism actually refutes moral relativism.

Dobson gives several reasons why moral relativism is what
he calls a "broken philosophy:"[14]

- Moral relativism is empty, meaningless, and pur-
  poseless. It can provide permission to do what
  should not be done or to tolerate what should not be
  tolerated, but it cannot provide hope. Nor can it give
  its proponents peace or answers to life's quandaries,
  problems, or mysteries.

- Moral relativism is self-refuting. The idea that there
  is no absolute truth—the cornerstone of moral relativism—is itself a declaration of absolute truth.

- People cling to moral relativism in the same way and
  for the same reason that smokers continue to smoke:
  they want what it does for them more than they want
  the benefits of quitting.[15]

Secular humanism is the religion of the Left. It has its
own bible, the *Humanist Manifesto*; its own ethical corollary,

moral relativism; and its own god, man. This is not just a clever ruse on the part of Christians to render the anti-religion views of secular humanism null and void. The *Humanist Manifesto* makes clear that secular humanism is a religion developed specifically to replace those religions of the world that are based on supernatural revelation. The facts are clear. Secular humanists do not oppose religion on campus, just the Christian religion. There is a name for this type of bias—religious bigotry—which brings us back to the case of Reverend Jeremiah Wright.

Obama's Relationship with the Reverend Jeremiah Wright

What undermines the President's credibility regarding his relationship with Reverend Jeremiah Wright is less about the Reverend's vitriolic anti-semitism and anti-Americanism and more about Obama's disingenuous and opportunistic handling of the controversy. When Reverend Wright's anti-semitism and anti-Americanism first became widely known as the result of a report on ABC News, Barack Obama attempted to straddle the fence in responding to inquiries about his pastor of twenty years. Clearly, he was trying to have his political cake and eat it too.

On one hand, he did not want to offend the portion of the African-American community that supported Reverend Wright. But on the other hand, he could not afford to lose the Jewish vote in his run for the presidency. Consequently, he initially responded by disclaiming Reverend Wright's intemperate remarks about "them Jews" while still endorsing him as a friend and pastor. When videos of Reverend Wright's vitriolic calls on God to "damn America" appeared, Obama claimed that Wright's comments had to be taken "in context." When this disingenuous ploy did not work, Obama turned his back on his pastor and walked away without looking back.

Even those who were sickened by Reverend Wright's anti-semitism and anti-Americanism questioned Obama's opportunistic and disingenuous handling of the controversy. Wright's views about those of the Jewish faith as well as his advocacy of liberation theology—a pseudo-Christian concept that is really just baptized Marxism—were not new. He had held and espoused these views for as long as Obama had been a member of his church. He and Obama were good friends. In fact, Wright even officiated at the wedding of Barack Obama to his wife, Michelle. The clear implication was that as long as Reverend Wright was a political asset, Obama valued his friendship, but as soon as he threatened to become a political liability, Obama cut him off and shut him out. To many Americans, this looked like what it was—a cold-blooded act of political expedience.

In the minds of many Americans, President Obama lost twice as a result of the Reverend Wright controversy. First, he lost because he maintained a close friendship with a person who held and espoused anti-semitic, anti-American views. Second, he lost because of how he handled the controversy once those views became a threat to his political ambitions. To many he appeared to be a heartless, deceitful political opportunist who would say anything and do anything to be President of the United States.

Obama, His Supporters, and the Military

One of the favorite targets of the Left—President Obama's most reliable base of support—is America's military. Attacking the military has long been a staple of the radical Left. Following the tragedy of the 9-11 terrorist attacks on the World Trade Center and the Pentagon, our country underwent what appeared to be a transformation. Liberals, conservatives, and moderates pulled together in a show of patriotism. "We Will Never Forget" bumper stickers could be seen displayed on the automobiles of people from both ends of the political spectrum. American flags were proudly displayed and the military was once again afforded a level of respect it had not enjoyed since the end of World War II. Unfortunately but not surprisingly, the national unity that resulted from the terrorist attacks of 9-11 did not last long. Many who claimed they would "never forget," forgot.

Following the 9-11 attacks, the radical left kept a low profile for awhile, perhaps fearing a pro-America backlash, or as is more likely the case, simply biding its time. Then in March of 2003, one of its foot soldiers—Nicholas DeGenova—broke the silence. DeGenova, a professor of anthropology and Latino studies at Columbia University, said during a teach-in that he hoped the United States military would suffer a "million Mogadishus."[16] In an attempt to defend his anti-military remark, DeGenova said:

> In my brief presentation, I outlined a long history of U.S. invasions, wars of conquest, military occupations, and colonization in order to establish that imperialism and white supremacy have been constitutive of U.S. nation-state formation and U.S. nationalism. In that context, I stressed the necessity of repudiating all forms of U.S. patriotism ... I emphasized that U.S. troops are indeed confronted with a choice— to perpetuate this war against the Iraqi people or to refuse to fight and contribute toward the defeat of the U.S. war machine.[17]

Campus Attacks on Military Recruiters

Among the Left's newest targets are military recruiters. Each branch of the military has a long history of visiting college and university campuses, setting up recruiting booths, and talking with students who might be interested in joining the military. Unfortunately, recruiters on left-wing campuses are easy targets for the obnoxious and even violent tactics of the radical Left. What follows are several examples of campus attacks on military recruiters led by the Campus Antiwar Network (CAN), a group affiliated with an organization called the Socialist Worker.

- "Members of the Campus Antiwar Network (CAN) at the Rochester Institute of Technology (RIT) are celebrating a significant victory after the director for Campus Life issued the order to stop allowing military recruiters in the Student Alumni Union...They may have been banned from the busiest place on campus, but they will find an alternative location to recruit. CAN has no problem with changing accommodations. We'll keep fighting."[18] Obviously, the radical left relishes its attacks on the military. Members of CAN created so much turmoil on the RIT campus that the institution's administration required recruiters to move to a remote location to avoid a riot. Notice it was the recruiters and not the perpetrators of the turmoil who were acted against by the university's administration. As can be seen from this example, the radical left is aggressively pursuing an anti-military agenda and university administrators are aiding and abetting their actions.

- San Francisco State University held a career fair on September 25, 2008. Among the participants were recruiters from the Marine Corps, Department of Homeland Security, and U.S. Border Patrol. In a direct attack on the military, student protesters marched on the recruiting booths shouting, "What are they recruiting for? Murder, rape, torture, and war." The protesters attempted to conduct a sit-in at the recruiting booths. When their attempts were foiled by police officers, they staged a rally outside the building. Eventually some of the protesters were able to gain admission to the building, at which point they harassed the Marine recruiters. [19]

• Anti-military students at Seattle Community College decided to shut down efforts by the military to recruit on campus in November 2008. Here is how Jorge Torres described the situation on the website of the Socialist Worker. "When activists in the Anti-War Collective and the International Socialist Organization heard two days ahead of time that Air Force, Army, and Coast Guard recruiters had all reserved tables in the school atrium for two hours during the busiest time of the day, they quickly publicized a protest by text messaging and passing out flyers. Some 20 students—some who were passing by—joined the action throughout the two hours. Students held picket signs, passed out fact sheets about the military and the lies recruiters tell, and chanted 'Recruiters off campus!'" [20]

Many Americans are appalled to see the military treated so disgracefully on college and university campuses. However, having served in the Marine Corps during the Vietnam War and experiencing firsthand some of the most violent of the antiwar, anti-military protests of that era, we know this is just the latest chapter in the Left's on-going war against the military. It did not stop after Vietnam. Rather, it simply went into temporary hibernation. The hibernation is over and the Left is back to attacking one of its favorite targets—the United States military.

The anti-military attitudes of President Obama's supporters—attitudes Obama has done and is doing nothing to challenge or change—are undermining his credibility with many Americans. Add to these attitudes President Obama's stated support for homosexuals in the military—social engineering that will undermine military morale and effectiveness—and his credibility suffers even more.

Anti-Christian, anti-military attitudes among his most ardent supporters cannot be swept under the rug and ignored by President Obama. He either agrees with his supporters or he doesn't. If he disagrees, he should step forward and say so. Political courage is what Americans are looking for in these troubled times, not political expedience. Obama cannot straddle the fence on religion or the military. Americans have a right to know where he stands on these two important issues. From his actions, it is clear that he does not stand on the Right.

NOTES

1. "Moral Relativism – Neutral Thinking?" Retrieved from http://www.moral-relativism.com on January 21, 2009, p.1.

2. Ibid.

3. As quoted in *Can America Survive?* By Ben Stein and Phil De-Muth (Carlsbad, CA: New Beginnings Press, an imprint of HAY HOUSE, Inc., 2004), 111.

4. "Moral Relativism – Neutral Thinking?" Retrieved from http://www.moral-relativism.com on January 21, 2009, 2.

5. As quoted in "Humanist Manifesto II." Retrieved from http://en.wikipedia.org/wiki/Humanist_Manifesto on January 21, 2009.

6. Ibid.

7. *Humanism and Its Aspirations* (American Humanist Association, Washington, D.C.:2003)

8. Perry L. Glanzer and Todd C. Ream, "Educating Different Types of Citizens: Identity, Tradition, Moral Education," *Journal of College & Character*, Vol. IX, No.4, April 2008, 1.

9. Anne Colby, "Whose Values Anyway?" *Journal of College & Character*, Retrieved from http://collegevalues.org/articles.cfm?a=1&id=685, p. 2.

10. Ibid, 3.

11. Ibid, 4.

12. Ryan Dobson, *Be Intolerant Because Some Things are Just Stupid* (Carol Stream, IL: Tyndale House Publishers, Inc., 2003), 55.

13. Ibid, 55-56.

14. Ibid, 49.

15. Ibid, 50-55.

16. "Nicolas DeGenova Explains What he Meant When he Called for a Million Mogadishus." Retrieved from http://hnn.us/articles/1396.html on January 29, 2009.

17. Ibid.

18. "Recruiters banned on RIT." Retrieved from http://socialistworker.org/2009/01/19recruiters-banned-at-RIT on January 30, 2009.

19. Kristin Lubbert, "Protesting the recruiters at SFSU." Retrieved from http://socialistworker.org/2009/09/29/protesting-recruiters-at-SFSU on January 30, 2009.

20. Jorge Torres, "Seattle protest against recruiters, *Activist News*. Retrieved from http://socialistworker.org/2008/12/02/seattle-protest-against-recruiters on January 30, 2009.

FIVE

Is President Obama an American?

*"President Obama is placing America on the
path of civilizational suicide...Washington
is poised to swallow the lethal pill
of global socialism."*

—Jeffrey T. Kuhner
The Washington Times, April 13, 2009

Of all the concerns expressed about President Obama, perhaps the greatest is that even if it turns out that he was an American at birth, he is still not an American at heart. Many Americans are concerned that their country—a country that built the most powerful economy in the history of the world on the basis of capitalism and entrepreneurship—now has a socialist in the Oval Office who is eager to work with fellow socialists in Congress. President Obama's policies and programs to date do nothing to dispel this concern.

In his book, *Welcome to Obamaland: I Have Seen your Future and it Doesn't Work*, British journalist James Delingpole sends an ominous message to all Americans. "This would be my first warning to you: if you think your new president and his... Democratic majorities in both houses of Congress can't do any serious harm to your vast, resilient country, that their socialist bromides might not, in the end, mark 'the end of the American idea' (to quote Mark Steyn)—well, you're quite wrong. Smiling socialists can do a great deal of damage indeed."[1]

Delingpole's book summarizes the state of Great Britain's

economy and British society in general in the wake of Tony Blair's socialist retreat from the hard-won reforms of Margaret Thatcher's administration. "Our economy is in ruins. We're afraid, and understandably so, for of all the G7 nations, our economy has officially been named the feeblest, the most out-of-control, and the one least likely to make a quick recovery from the global depression." [2]   His observations about British society during the Blair administration paint an even bleaker picture:

- Knife and gun crime was up

- Food and fuel costs were skyrocketing

- The railroad system was collapsing

- Hospitals were filthy and overcrowded

- School standards were plummeting

- British universities were becoming a joke [3]

Delingpole describes how the everyday freedoms of British citizens in "the world's oldest democracy were increasingly circumscribed by petty, micromanaging, nanny-ish laws governing every aspect of our behavior from the games our kids could play at school, to the kind of light bulbs we could use, to how often we could dispose of our trash, to the sort of jokes it was permissible to tell. We'd gone, in a terrifyingly short space, from being a thriving capitalist state to a failed socialist experiment."[4]

What is Socialism?

Because President Obama and his leftist supporters can so nonchalantly pass socialistic laws, programs, and policies without raising so much as a word of caution from his fawning press corps, we believe it is important to include herein what some readers may consider a remedial civics lesson. If some of what is presented in this chapter is old information to you, we apologize at the outset and recommend that you use this information for educating the less informed in your circle of friends and acquaintances. After all, there must be plenty of these ill-informed Americans scattered around the country— Obama was elected.

If defined strictly from an economic perspective, socialism is a centrally-planned economy in which the government controls all of the means of production, distribution, and commerce and seeks to make all people economically and socially equal. However, defining socialism as simply an economic system falls well short of full disclosure. Socialism is more than just an economic system. It is an economic system that is part of a broader worldview—a worldview in which God is replaced by the state and the power of government is used to take from productive people and give to those who are less productive. We begin this section by explaining the economic perspective of socialism. Then, later in this section we explain the broader worldview aspects of the concept.

Robert Heilbroner, a socialist for most his life before seeing the light, describes socialism as "the tragic failure of the twentieth century."[5] Originally envisioned as a remedy for what was viewed by some as the defects of capitalism, socialism has failed dismally everywhere it has been tried. Writing about socialism, Heilbroner says:

> [I]t has far surpassed capitalism in both economic malfunction and moral cruelty. Yet the idea and the ideal of socialism linger on. Whether socialism in some form will eventually return as a major organizing force in human

affairs is unknown, but no one can accurately appraise its prospects who has not taken into account the dramatic story of its rise and fall." [6]

Socialism: The Historical Perspective

Socialism's birth is typically attributed to Karl Marx but, in fact, he wrote only a few pages about the concept in his well-known work, *The Communist Manifesto.* In the modern era, advocates of socialism included Robert Owen, Charles Fourier, Pierre-Joseph Proudon, Louis Blanc, Charles Hall, and Saint-Simon. This group criticized what they saw as the inequities of the Industrial Revolution. To remedy those perceived inequities they advocated a more egalitarian redistribution of wealth and a reordering of society into small utopian communities in which there would be no private property.

Socialistic thinking has dominated in Europe—as well as in many quarters in America—since the late 19th century. Socialists throughout Europe dominated the universities, influenced the thinking of intellectuals, and encouraged the spread of socialism in every way possible. The Fabian Socialists of England were especially effective in bringing democratic socialism to that country. They also influenced socialist thought in America. The Fabians sought to bring about the acceptance and spread of socialism by gradual means, beginning with scholarly works on economic history, and using popular literature to influence public opinion. Working in tandem with other socialist groups, the Fabians played a key role in the establishment of the British welfare state.

In the United States, socialism was prominent in the thinking of rationalistic New England and Northern reformers. For example, the first "free" public schools were established by Unitarian socialists who wanted to use them as a vehicle for undermining Christianity, changing America's cultural values, and promoting the acceptance of socialism. 19th and 20th century immigration, particularly from Germany, brought a wave of socialists and socialist intellectuals to America. In the process, classical, small-government liberalism was transformed into big-government democratic socialism.

Nationalistic socialists of the 1880s and 1890s, like the Fabian socialists, sought to achieve the spread of socialism gradually and peacefully through increased government control of industries. Arguing that political equality is meaningless without economic equality, they had a powerful influence on many middle-class Americans. At the same time, Christian Socialism and the Social Gospel influenced many Christians in the old main-line Protestant denominations from the 1880s through the 1920s. Those who were influenced by the Social Gospel attacked business, supported organized labor, and promoted the notion that social justice requires economic equality.

In politics, the 1890s and 1900s saw the emergence and growth in America of the Socialist Party and the Socialist Labor Party. The "Progressives" of the early 20th century were strongly influenced by socialism. Consequently, they expected government to exercise more control over business, and adopted—to some extent—socialist programs. Intellectuals in politics used their influence to encourage the acceptance and spread of socialism during these years. For example, President Woodrow Wilson—the former college professor and college president—advanced socialist thinking through his teaching, public oratory, and policies during World War I.

Later, Franklin Roosevelt, with help from his left-wing "Brain Trust", a Democrat-controlled Congress, and *me-too* Republicans, laid the foundation for American socialism with his New Deal policies, programs, and Supreme Court appointments. Subsequent presidents, Congresses, and liberal Supreme Court majorities—aided and abetted by left-wing intellectuals in colleges, universities, and the entertainment industry—slowly but steadily advanced the spread of socialism in America. There was opposition, of course. But as it always does when opposition arises, the Left deftly applied the concept of boiling the frog so that progress was slow enough to go unnoticed by the majority of Americans.

Socialism really got a boost when it was adopted by Lenin following the Russian Revolution in which Czar Nicholas was overthrown and his family murdered. Having defeated the Russian aristocracy, Lenin's now-powerful followers had a free hand and no need to compromise with political opponents. Socialists everywhere applauded Lenin's—and socialism's—ascension to power and eagerly awaited the results of what they referred to as the "great experiment."

Having seized power in Russia, Lenin found himself in the uncomfortable position of having to follow through on his promises to make things better. Lenin believed that a nation's economy would perform better with centralized state control of production, distribution, and commerce and without what he thought of as the negative influences of the profit motive and competition. Predictably, Lenin's attempt to apply socialist principles on a broad scale failed miserably. Just four years after the institution of a socialist economy, production in the Soviet Union had fallen to only a fraction of its rate prior to the revolution. In fact, Lenin's experiment was such an abysmal failure that he was forced to choose between the Soviet people starving and reinstituting the free-market incentives of capitalism, albeit on a limited basis. He opted for limited capitalism under what was called the *New Economic Program* (NEP).

This is where things stood when Lenin died and Stalin

assumed the reins of power. Stalin and his successors, until the collapse of the Soviet Union, based the country's economy on state planning of production based on a pyramid model. At the peak of the pyramid, the state planning agency established broad targets and directives. These targets and directives cascaded down through a succession of ministries and regional planning organizations that, in turn, passed them down to factories. In the factories, the plans were reviewed by the factory managers and engineers who were expected to implement them. [7]

Lenin's misguided experiment with socialism stumbled along for approximately 70 years—a textbook example of mass inefficiency and waste—until the Soviet Union's socialist economy gasped its last breath and finally collapsed. Without massive and repeated infusions of economic aid from the United States and the countries of Western Europe in the form of technology and expertise—including factories and the technicians to run them—the failure of the "great experiment" would have occurred much sooner.

Heilbroner describes the collapse of the Soviet Union's doomed socialist economy in stark terms:

> It is not surprising that this increasingly Byzantine system began to create serious dysfunctions beneath the overall statistics of growth. During the 1960s the Soviet Union became the first industrial country in history to suffer a prolonged peacetime fall in average life expectancy, a symptom of its disastrous misallocation of resources. Military research facilities could get whatever they needed, but hospitals were low on the priority list. By the 1970s the figures clearly indicated a slowing

of overall production. By the 1980s the Soviet
Union officially acknowledged a near end
to growth that was, in reality, an unofficial
decline. In 1987 the first official law embodying
perestroika—restructuring—was put into effect.
President Mikhail Gorbachev announced
his intention to revamp the economy from
top to bottom by introducing the market,
reestablishing private ownership, and opening
the system to free economic interchange with
the West. Seventy years of socialist rise had
come to an end."[8]

Socialism has been tried many times by many different nations over many years. Throughout all of this, it has been consistent in its record of failure. Christian philosopher D. Elton
Trueblood demonstrated that a centrally-planned economy requires the planners to know: 1) what resources are immediately
available, 2) what resources will be available in the future, 3)
what consumers want now, and 4) what consumers will want in
the future.[9] Of course, this means that central planners must
be aware of market factors that are impossible to know—factors that only God can know. In a free-market economy, factors
such as prices, profits, and losses are immediately available and
provide businesses the information needed to respond quickly
to market opportunities and threats, to change their plans in
response to the ever-changing conditions of the market. This
is one of the reasons why a free-market economy works more
efficiently than a socialist economy.

Socialism as a Worldview

Socialism is a failed concept even when viewed strictly from
the perspective of economics. However, when viewed in the

broader context of a worldview, the truth about this unworkable concept becomes even more disturbing. In order to accept the socialist worldview, you must accept the premise that the state knows better than the individual how people should live and what people should believe. The highest authority to a socialist is the all-knowing, all-powerful, all-authoritative state. In other words, to a socialist the state is god. As god, the state controls all aspects of life. Just as Christians worship the one true and Holy God of the Bible, socialists worship the state.

This state-as-god mentality is why socialists willingly submit to centralized government control of not just the economy, but all aspects of their lives—what people should believe, how people should live, and what people should think. Hence, socialism is a religious philosophy based on faith in man's providence; a worldview that replaces God's divine providence with faith in man's ability to ensure his own salvation. Faith is the substance of things hoped for and the proof of things unseen, and faith is why socialists stubbornly cling to their misguided views in spite of the concept's long record of failure.

Practical Flaws of Socialism

As an economic system, socialism is a flawed concept. Consider just a few of the inherent shortcomings of this ill-conceived notion. Socialism does not, will not, and cannot work because it:

- Appeals to the base aspects of human nature

- Replaces the family as the central unit in society with the state

- Allows legalized theft in the name of redistribution of wealth to achieve "social justice"

- Encourages sloth instead of diligence

- Rewards irresponsibility, laziness, and a lack of accountability

- Encourages self-indulgence instead of self-reliance

- Encourages the shifting of responsibility to others

- Replaces the self-discipline of delayed gratification with the desire for instant gratification

- Undermines all aspects of the traditional work ethic (*i.e.* thrift, diligence, self-reliance, self-discipline, responsibility, accountability, deferred gratification, and hard work) and replaces them with an entitlement mentality

- Treats those who contribute to the betterment of society the same—worse, in fact, because it takes from them what they have earned—as those who do not, even when they are capable of doing so

- Promotes a get-something-for-nothing mentality that undermines the moral character of the individual and society

- Robs people of initiative, drive, and ambition as well as wealth

- Undermines the spirit of entrepreneurship and competitiveness

- Promotes totalitarianism, thereby undermining freedom and liberty

In a radio broadcast prior to the British general election of 1945, Winston Churchill said this about socialism: "A socialist policy is abhorrent to the British ideas of freedom. Socialism is inseparably interwoven with totalitarianism and...worship of the state. It will prescribe for everyone where they are to work, what they are to work at, where they may go and what they may say. Socialism is an attack on the right to breathe freely." [10]

Scriptural Flaws of Socialism

As flawed as socialism is when viewed strictly as an economic system, it fares even worse as a worldview. What follows are some of the scriptural flaws of socialism:

- Violates the First Commandment by replacing God with the state. As part of its state-as-god perspective, socialism replaces God's never-changing laws with man's ever-changing social mores, or with the desires of socialist manipulators concerning man's mores.

- Violates the Second Commandment in that it worships man and idolizes his fickle desires.

- Violates the Third Commandment by advocating man's right to blaspheme God or to profess Christ while simultaneously promoting laws and practices that violate God's law.

- Violates the Fourth Commandment by denigrating God's admonition to work six days while keeping the Sabbath holy and reserving the day for worship, rest, and fellowship. It also denigrates work by treating idlers in the same way as productive people who contribute more to society.

- Violates the Fifth Commandment by undermining families, undercutting parental authority, attacking traditional marriage, and supporting laws that enable the state to take that which should be passed from generation to generation by inheritance.

• Violates the Sixth Commandment by legalizing murder in the forms of abortion, infanticide, and euthanasia, all of which have been or are legally practiced in socialist countries, and all of which are supported by the Left and Obama.

• Violates the Seventh Commandment by replacing the definition of justice from God's Law with "social justice" or equality of income and wealth, and by legalizing theft through taxation under the banner of redistributing wealth.

• Violates the Eighth Commandment by de facto condoning adultery with policies and practices that promote sexual promiscuity and indiscriminate sexual indulgence.

• Violates the Ninth Commandment by promoting class warfare that leads to the bearing of false witness against neighbors (*e.g.* portraying the wealthy as exploiters of the poor, using political rhetoric that promotes class envy and strife).

• Violates the Tenth Commandment by promoting covetousness through class envy, advocating the redistribution of wealth, and encouraging an entitlement mentality.

Denying the Evidence of Socialism's Inherent Fundamental Flaws

As they push the government ever closer to nationalizing banks, automobile manufacturers, insurance companies, healthcare, education, and energy production, left-leaning politicians are ignoring incontrovertible evidence of the inherent flaws of socialism. Socialism cannot work in a world where the ability to compete in the global arena is so large a factor in determining a nation's quality of life. It does not and cannot work because of three inherent and irreversible flaws: 1) it presupposes that man rather than God governs history, 2) it presupposes that God will not judge socialist societies and governments for violating his holy laws, and 3) it appeals to the worst aspects of human nature. For evidence of this fact, one need only look at the situation that now exists in Europe as a result of socialist government policies and the socialist mindset of the people.

Britain is not alone in allowing socialism to hold it back in the battle of the marketplace waged every day by the competitive nations of the world. Because of their socialist economies, European countries are like sprinters who must drag an anchor behind them as they race against fleet, unencumbered runners from India, China, Japan, and Korea. Britain and the other European nations have descended into socialism and, despite the disastrous results brought by this failed concept, America is blindly following their lead. Socialism has failed everywhere it has been tried and yet left-leaning politicians continue to promote it. What these politicians refuse to acknowledge is that socialism fails because it is inherently flawed, not because Europeans have failed to effectively apply its principles.

> According to a recent study by the Organization for Economic Cooperation and Development, the average working American spends 1,976

hours a year on the job. The average German works just 1,535—22 percent less. The Dutch and Norwegians put in even fewer hours. Even the British do 10 percent less work than their trans-Atlantic cousins. Even these figures understate the extent of European idleness, because a larger proportion of Americans work. Unemployment rates in most Northern European countries are also markedly higher than those in the United States. Then there are the strikes. Between 1992 and 2001, the Spanish economy lost, on average, 271 days per 1,000 employees as a result of strikes. For Denmark, Italy, Finland, Ireland and France, the figures range between 80 and 120 days.[11]

Consider how these facts play out in the global arena. While Europeans are idle, workers in Japan, China, India, and Korea are producing. To make matters worse, even when they are working Europeans are less productive than their Asian competitors because of their poor work ethic.

Capitalism works—albeit imperfectly—because it is more consistent with God's Word than other systems and because it appeals to and rewards many of the positive elements of human nature, biblical character, and Christian values (*i.e.* thrift, diligence, self-reliance, self-discipline, responsibility, accountability, delayed gratification, and hard work as well as initiative, ambition, perseverance, entrepreneurship, etc.). Socialism does not work because it violates God's law and because it appeals to and rewards the sinful elements of human nature (*i.e.* sloth, laziness, dependence on others, irresponsibility, lack of ambition, covetousness, etc.). Capitalism rewards those who pull the wagon. Socialism rewards those who ride in it. Those on the Left who deny this inherent flaw of socialism are blinded by political bias and partisan prejudice. They think that socialism will work simply because they want it to.

Using False Compassion to Convince Americans of Socialism's Viability

One of the most effective tools used by the Left to sell socialism to the American public is compassion—false compassion. This is President Obama's principal strategy in trying to win support for his healthcare plan. Aided and abetted by the media, the Left claims to be more compassionate toward the "victims" of society—a message that plays well to Americans encouraged by teachers, trial lawyers, and government bureaucrats to view themselves as victims. However, the truth is that conservatives give a much higher percentage of their personal income to charity than do liberals. For a complete accounting of this little-known fact, see *Who Really Cares: The Surprising Truth about Compassionate Conservatism* (New York: Basic Books, 2006) by Arthur C. Brooks.

In fact, with the assistance of the media and civil trial lawyers, liberals have turned victimhood into one of America's most prosperous industries. Unfortunately, the so-called compassion of the Left is the type that gives in to the alcoholic who begs for a drink or the addict who pleads for a fix. Giving in will feed the need for the moment, but makes the addiction worse in the long run. The unavoidable result of this advocacy of victimhood is the encouragement of dependence and entitlement.

The Left has mastered the art of *compassion rhetoric* and uses it effectively to sell socialism to a gullible American public in much the same way a snake-oil salesman hawks his wares. One of the Left's favorite terms for selling socialism is *equality*.

"Equality" has become the mantra of the Left. After all, didn't Thomas Jefferson advocate equality for all men in the Declaration of Independence? Didn't Jefferson say that "all men are created equal?" Historians still debate whether Jefferson meant that all men are created equal before God or before the law. But there are no serious scholars who believe he meant what the Left means by equality: *equality of outcome rather than opportunity.* The Left advocates, legislates, and intimidates in its on-going attempts to guarantee equality of outcomes in society regardless of merit or effort. Anyone on the Right who dares claim that an unproductive member of society deserves less than a productive member is quickly labeled "hard-hearted" or "mean-spirited."

The Left also likes to use the term *fairness* when selling socialism. However, the Left's deliberately vague definition of *fairness* clearly violates God's definition of the term. God's law—the only perfect and unchanging standard—prohibits civil government as well as anyone else, rich or poor, from engaging in legalized theft. Since civil government is supposed to be a ministry of God, a function of which is to protect those who do good from those who do evil (Romans 13), civil government—more than any other entity—is prohibited from engaging in theft.

Although most of the politicians who promote big-government and socialism are themselves quite wealthy, they like to play the class card when arguing for socialism. They pit the so-called "haves" of society against the "have-nots," conveniently ignoring their own status as haves. Their favorite tactic is to portray the *haves* as ogres and the *have-nots* as victims regardless of how long and hard the *haves* had to work for the material success they now enjoy or how much their work has benefitted others. The radical Left—Obama's most reliable support base—

claims it is "unfair" for a thrifty, diligent, self-reliant producer, who pulls America's economic wagon, to have more than a lazy, irresponsible, entitled person who only rides in the wagon.

Using Emotionalism to Sell Americans on Socialism

Next to false compassion, emotionalism is the most effective tool of President Obama and his supporters for selling socialism to a gullible American public, and healthcare is the issue around which they build their most emotional arguments. Socialists believe that healthcare should be free and universally available to everyone regardless of their ability to pay. "Free" universal healthcare is the five-hundred pound gorilla on the list of President Obama's most important issues. And you have to hand it to the Left, on the surface this is an appealing concept. Few things are closer to the hearts of Americans than their health and the health of their loved ones.

This is why emotionalism is such an effective tool for socialists pushing the universal healthcare agenda. But there is a problem here that socialists like to ignore. Nothing is free, and especially not healthcare. In fact, few things are more expensive than healthcare. Even with all of its abundance, America has finite resources. There are simply not sufficient resources in this or any other country to provide high-quality universal healthcare that is paid for by taxpayers. When economists point out this undeniable fact, socialists immediately fall back on emotionalism and portray the naysayers as "hard-hearted" capitalists who don't care about their fellow human beings. This is an excellent example of a key difference between a socialist and a capitalist. Socialists envision a utopian world and think it can happen simply because that is how they want it to be. Capitalists are better students of human nature. Consequently, they temper their dreams with reality.

One of the realities capitalists always keep in mind is limited resources. Any time there are limited resources, decisions must be made and sometimes they can be hard decisions. In every other aspect of our lives, most people understand that those who can afford more in the way of material advantages will have them; this is the nature of life. But socialists like to play the class card and label this fact of life as unfair. Putting aside the fact that life itself is unfair because of man's sinful nature, what is wrong with an individual who contributes more to the economy being able to secure better healthcare in the same way he is able to secure a bigger house and nicer car? After all, even socialists understand this concept.

For example, ask yourself where the wealthy politicians in Washington, D.C. live, what kind of cars they drive, and where they send their children to school. What is any different about healthcare? The answer to this question is simple: *emotional appeal.* Healthcare appeals to people on such an emotional level that wealthy leftists can use it to build an ever-growing constituent base of poor people by questioning the fairness of a system that treats the rich and the poor differently. The hard truth—and socialists do not like hard truths—is that when you have universal demand, but finite resources, the fairest system is the free-market system.

What the emotionalism of socialists conveniently glosses over is that in its own imperfect way, the free-market system results in better healthcare for the poor, the wealthy, and those in the middle—just as it results in better cars, homes, food, and everything else needed by human beings. On the most fundamental level, the free-market system gives people the incentive to improve themselves economically so they and their families can enjoy better healthcare, homes, cars, foods, and all of the other human necessities. Socialism, on the other hand, provides no such incentives. Why work hard to improve your economic circumstances when you have a "right" to the same socio-economic advantages as someone who contributes more to society and the economy?

Socialists despise the logic contained in this question. Consequently, upon hearing it they typically respond with their favorite knee-jerk comeback—one that is virtually dripping with emotional appeal: "You think you are better than everyone else." The relative worth of individual human beings is not even the issue here. Christians know that we all stand equally unclothed before God as sinners, which is precisely why it is best to let the free market, rather than the state, make difficult economic choices for us. When the free market chooses, the issue is not who is better than whom but who has worked long, hard, and smart enough to achieve sufficient wealth to be able to afford more.

Of course, there are people whose wealth is inherited, people who have done nothing to deserve the advantages they enjoy in a free-market system. In fact, many of them are left-leaning politicians who hypocritically push a socialist agenda—Senators Ted Kennedy and John Kerry come to mind. Advocates of socialist programs like to use emotionalism to claim it is unfair that a poor person receive less of some human necessity than a wealthy person. According to socialists, this is just not fair. However, these same socialists are unable to explain why they think it is fair that someone who contributes less to the economy should be entitled to the same benefits as someone who contributes more.

Left-leaning politicians such as President Obama and his supporters claim to be more compassionate than free-market proponents, but their emotional appeals for "fairness" are just empty words. If they really wanted to be fair, they would be more charitable with their own substantial wealth, rather than taxing middle-income Americans who work hard to provide for themselves and their families. It is easy to be "compassionate" with someone else's money. But where is the fairness when Left-leaning politicians live in the most exclusive neighborhoods and send their children to the best private schools while taxing hard-working Americans, who can neither live in those neighborhoods nor send their children to those private schools? This is the hypocrisy of President Obama and his supporters.

Government as an Instrument of Socialist Control

Christians have faith in God, but socialists have faith only in the state. In fact, to a socialist the state is god. This misguided faith in government is difficult to comprehend until one understands the ultimate goal of socialists—complete control. Socialists seek to control every aspect of life, and to a socialist the state is the ultimate instrument of control. Mark Levin, author of *Liberty and Tyranny: A Conservative Manifesto*, explains how socialists seek to control America by building a "culture of conformity and dependency, where the ideal citizen takes on drone-like qualities in service to the state, the individual must be drained of uniqueness and self-worth, and deterred from independent thought or behavior."[12]

History and experience show that big government is inherently inefficient. The reason for this inefficiency goes beyond size—although students of organizational behavior know that big is typically synonymous with inefficient. Even in the private sector, organizations tend to lose efficiency as they grow. However, the private sector at least has the marketplace to enforce fiscal discipline. The government, on the other hand, is ruled by politics not markets, and politics is the least-disciplined concept known to man.

As President Obama and his supporters continue to push

America down the slippery slope into socialism, as the federal government continues to grow and the federal debt continues to spiral out of control, the types of productivity-sapping inefficiencies associated with the former Soviet Union are beginning to be seen in the United States. This is how Mark Levin describes America's rapidly-growing, increasingly-centralized government: "It administers a budget of over $3 trillion. It churns out a mind-numbing number of rules that regulate energy, the environment, business, labor, employment, transportation, housing, agriculture, food, drugs, education, etc. Even the slightest human activity apparently requires its intervention: clothing labels on women's dresses, cosmetic ingredients, and labeling. It even reaches into the bathroom, mandating showerhead flow rates and allowable gallons per flush for toilets. It sets flammability standards for beds." [13]

This intrusive, oppressive approach to governing is what excites socialists. They see it as their most effective means of control, and it certainly is that. The type of oppressive government that socialists advocate undermines initiative, ambition, free-thought, the work ethic, freedom, liberty, and the entrepreneurial spirit. This is why so many people question if President Obama is really an American at heart. Even the most liberal presidents in the past have not advocated oppressive government that undermines the very freedom, attitude, and spirit that made America great.

Among the many problems associated with big government, one stands out above the rest: it does not work. James Delingpole uses Great Britain's National Health System to make this point:

> Quite simply, government can never run any service as efficiently as private enterprise can. For one thing, it operates on a scale too

unwieldy. The British National Health Service is the world's largest employer after the Chinese army and the Indian State Railway... In 2007-2008 the British National Health Service swallowed up 95 billion pounds—more than any other government department. For this, the taxpayer gets a "service" so lamentably poor that 55 percent of senior doctors pay for private medical insurance rather than run the risk of having to expose themselves to the NHS's tender care.[14]

The Blind Faith of President Obama and His Supporters in Socialism

The evidence of socialism's failure is conclusive and undeniable to any objective observer. Why then do socialists cling so stubbornly to their *state-as-god* mentality? Of course, socialists are anything but objective observers, but the reasons behind their stubborn adherence to socialist orthodoxy go well beyond a lack of objectivity. David Limbaugh calls this socialist mentality "beltway arrogance and blind faith."[15] Socialists criticize Christians for having what they describe as "blind faith in God," yet President Obama and his supporters cling to their socialist notions—in spite of their perfect record of failure—out of blind faith. Limbaugh cites the example of Congressman Charles Rangel, one of the Left's most vocal champions of socialist programs: "Rep. Charles Rangel's recent comments about President Obama's budget exemplify the liberal ruling class's Beltway arrogance and blind faith in an ideology that compels it to press on the accelerator as we head for the cliff toward the nation's financial ruin."[16]

In an interview with Chris Wallace on *Fox News Sunday,*

Representative Rangel claimed that he was not troubled by a report from the Congressional Budget Office estimating that President Obama's federal budget deficit would be $2.3 trillion higher than the already astronomically-high projections of the White House. According to Limbaugh, what Rangel meant by his lack of concern was that: "We liberals are going to do what we have been itching to do for decades, and even though our policies will place even greater burdens on the economy, retard economic growth, and cause the debt and deficits to further explode, we'll end up with a surplus anyway because we are so doggone virtuous with our liberal compassion that fate will have to reward us."[17]

Arrogance, false compassion, emotionalism, and blind faith in a system that not only does not work but breeds laziness, sloth, and irresponsibility—these are the characteristics necessary to accept President Obama's socialist programs. Until America replaces these characteristics with those that make up the traditional work ethic—thrift, diligence, self-reliance, self-discipline, responsibility, accountability, and hard work—all government programs in the world will have no more effect than water that is poured into a leaky bucket. In the age of global competition, America cannot win with an inefficient, government-controlled leaky bucket.

Socialists claim to want to help people, but their claim cannot stand up to the scrutiny of either logic or common sense. An objective observer might ask, "How do you help the poor by hurting the rich?" or "How do you help the jobless by hurting the entrepreneurs who create the jobs?" In truth, the best way to help someone is to empower him to help himself. America's 26th president, Teddy Roosevelt, was the personification of the work ethic that helped make America great. He summarized his thoughts on government sponsored programs that undermine the work ethic when he said: "The only permanently beneficial way in which to help anyone is to help him help himself; if either private charity, or governmental action, or any form of social expression destroys the individual's power of self-help, the gravest possible wrong is really done the individual."[18]

Socialism does the "gravest possible wrong" to the individual because it undermines the character traits most likely to ensure a productive life that contributes to the betterment of society: thrift, diligence, self-reliance, self-discipline, responsibility, accountability, and hard work. Arrogantly undermining the character of America is precisely what President Obama and his supporters are doing, and will continue to do, until Americans finally say "enough is enough" and take their country back from those bent on destroying it.

NOTES

1. James Delingpole, *Welcome to Obamaland: I have Seen Your Future and It Doesn't Work* (Washington, DC: Regnery Publishing, Inc., 2009), 2.

2. Ibid, 3.

3. Ibid.

4. Ibid.

5. Robert Heilbroner, "Socialism," Library of Economics and Liberty. Retrieved from http://www.econlib.org/libary/Enc/Socialism.html on March 26, 2009.

6. Ibid.

7. Ibid.

8. Ibid.

9. D. Elton Trueblood, Retrieved from http://www.waynet.org/people/biography/trueblood.htm on August 8, 2009.

10. Quoted in Alan O. Ebenstein, *Friedrich Hayek: A Biography* (University of Chicago Press, Chicago: 2003), 137.

11. Niall Ferguson, "The World: Why America Outpaces Europe," *The New York Times.* Retrieved from http://query. nytimes.com/gst/fullpage.html?res=9D04E3D91739F93BA3 5755C0A9659C8 on December 12, 2008.

12. Mark R. Levin, As quoted by Eli Lake in "Levin's manifesto declares war on the statists," *Washington Times,* March 30, 2009, 26.

13. Ibid.

14. Delingpole, *Welcome to Obamaland: I have Seen Your Future and It Doesn't Work,* 43.

15. David Limbaugh, "Beltway arrogance and blind faith," *Washington Times,* March 30, 2009, 37.

16. Ibid.

17. Ibid.

18. President Theodore Roosevelt as quoted in "He's no Teddy Roosevelt," by Marvin Olasky, *World Magazine,* April 11, 2009.

CONCLUSIONS

Truth and Trust Versus
Arrogance and Deceit

In this book we have tried to introduce common sense and reason into a debate that has been characterized by *ad hominem* arguments, mean-spirited name-calling, stereotypical labeling, and belittling comments from sources both predictable and not so predictable. In the process, we have arrived at a number of conclusions that are summarized herein:

- The questions about Barack Obama's citizenship represent a serious Constitutional issue that deserves a closer, more objective examination than it has received thus far. These questions are inconvenient—due in part to the historical significance of Obama's election as America's first African-American president—but they are important nonetheless and deserve satisfactory answers. Simply brushing a Constitutional issue aside as President Obama has, claiming that his detractors will never be satisfied with any proof of citizenship, is nothing more than clever political spin. For decades African-Americans endured the type of prejudicial thinking that lumped them all together only to have the first African-American president apply the same type of bias to his detractors.

- The Constitutional issue at the heart of the birth-
  certificate debate is of paramount importance. If
  American citizens must produce a birth certificate in
  order to enroll in school, play Little League baseball,
  or get a driver's license, why shouldn't a politician
  who wants to be president have to do the same?

- It does matter that President Obama or any other
  American president be a natural-born citizen. The
  founders of our country were appropriately concerned when drafting Article II, Section 1, Clause
  5 of the Constitution that no person with divided
  loyalties be allowed to serve as president. Their
  concerns at the time were that an individual who
  might be more loyal to a European nation than to
  the United States would be elected president. They
  knew the biblical admonition about a house divided
  against itself and they also knew that electing a
  president with divided loyalties was the fastest way
  to end up with such a house. This concern is just as
  relevant today—and perhaps even more so in the age
  of globalization—than it was at the founding of our
  nation.

- President Obama's disingenuous and even imperious
  handling of the citizenship issue fuels the flames of
  controversy. Like many Americans, including some
  of his supporters, we do not understand why he
  refuses to unlock his records and put an end to the
  questions. That is, of course, unless he has something to hide.

- Lumping together all doubters and labeling them
  as conspiracy-theorists, sore losers, and racists is

a defense unworthy of the President of the United States. President Obama ran as a Democrat and was fairly elected by a clear, albeit small, majority of American voters. He was elected not as president of the Democrat party, but rather as President of the United States. As such, he has a moral obligation to all Americans—supporters and detractors—to be open, honest, and transparent. Lumping together doubters and labeling them in a pejorative way may be clever politics, but it is not presidential leadership.

- Politically expedient Republicans and conservative commentators who would like the birth-certificate doubters to forget the issue and go away, are just as wrong as Obama's Left-leaning supporters. Conservatives who actually stoop to the name-calling tactics of the Left when attacking doubters are even worse than Obama's most ardent and vitriolic supporters, who think the President is above being held accountable by the American public. Those who place a higher priority on political expedience than issues of presidential and Constitutional integrity, do not deserve the offices they hold or the microphones they use to make a living.

- The volume and content of the name-calling directed at doubters is, itself, telling. Anytime someone resorts to attacking the questioner rather than simply answering the question, something is amiss. Often what is amiss is that the person has something to hide.

- The controversy over President Obama's birth certificate is not likely to ever gain a hearing before Con-

gress or the courts, which is a disappointing fact that
borders on dereliction of duty. But eventually every
president in a democratic society must stand before
the ultimate tribunal: the court of public opinion.
Unless he is willing to open his life and records to
public scrutiny as every other elected official must
do, President Obama will eventually be called to account by the court of public opinion. After all, he is
an elected official, not a king or a czar. The President
of the United States is not exempt from obeying the
same laws that are obligatory for all American citizens.

• Leadership is about change and President Obama
  ran on a platform of change. However, change can
  be discomfiting for people. Consequently, leaders
  always face the challenge of generating support for
  the changes they propose. In order to win support,
  they must first build trust. People will not follow
  a leader they do not trust. In order to win trust, a
  leader must convince the people that he has their
  best interests at heart and that the changes he pro-
  poses will make their lives better. Obama has failed
  to win the trust of a substantial and growing portion
  of the American people. Consequently, he has had
  to resort to political force in the form of blatant par-
  tisanship to move his programs for change through
  Congress, and even with his party in control Obama
  is finding it difficult to make headway.

• There are numerous issues undermining the trust of
  the American public in President Obama including:
  the moving target of healthcare reform with its as-

tronomical price tag and threats to both quality and
access, waffling on tax increases, racialism as seen in
the Cambridge Police incident that led to the "Beer
Summit," his past associations with such individuals
as Frank Marshall Davis and the Reverend Jeremiah
Wright, the broken promise of non-partisanship,
hypocritical secrecy concerning visits to the White
House by executives from the healthcare and insurance industries, the broken promise about televising
the healthcare debates on C-SPAN, his chummy
standing with left-leaning European leaders, the naiveté of his open-hand approach to foreign relations,
historical revisionism on the subject of America's
Christian heritage, and hostility toward the military.

• President Obama has failed to earn credibility
with many Americans. In order to have credibility, a leader must convince the people that he: 1)
cares about them, 2) knows what he is doing, 3)
knows where he is trying to lead them, and 4) is
trying to lead them to an appropriate destination.
Further, if a leader is going to have credibility,
those he hopes to lead must be able to relate to
him in a positive way. One of the reasons so many
Americans cannot relate to President Obama is his
apparent negativity on two issues that are important to them: religion and the military. Obama's
association with Reverend Jeremiah Wright, his
comments about the United States being one of
the largest Muslim nations in the world, his endorsement of the concepts of secular humanism
and moral relativism, his views on homosexuals
in the military, and his weakening of our military

capability have combined to undermine his credibility with many Americans.

- The bottom-line issue for many Americans is the
  belief that even if he turns out to be an American by
  birth, he is not an American at heart. Although all of
  the information summarized in the previous conclusions provides abundant evidence of this concern,
  the principal factor behind this belief is President
  Obama's endorsement of socialism. With Obama,
  nationalizing private businesses is just another day
  at the office. He apparently thinks nothing of turning the federal government into a gigantic non-profit
  corporation drowning in debt. For President Obama,
  government is the answer not the problem, but for
  many Americans the obverse is true. Even many of
  his supporters, other than those on the far Left, are
  appalled at the President's propensity for adopting
  socialist ideals that have nothing to recommend them
  but a long and consistent record of failure.

- Barack Obama raised his right hand, swore an oath,
  and became President of the United States at a critical juncture in America's history. When he took
  office, our country was engaged in an on-going war
  on terrorism, we were dependent for oil on nations
  that despise everything we hold most dear, our
  economy was in its worst condition since the Great
  Depression, race relations were tense at best, and
  enemies bent on our destruction were circling like
  sharks. There have been few times in the history of
  our nation when strong leadership, a clear vision,
  unquestionable transparency, and certain trust have

been more badly needed. Instead, with President Obama, America got arrogance, deceit, and broken promises in domestic affairs, and in foreign affairs we got apologies, naiveté, and a weakened military.

• Being the first African-American elected as President of the United States is an accomplishment of historic significance and monumental proportions, one of which all Americans—supporters of Obama as well as opponents—should be proud. But the historical significance of his election, as important as it is, will not pull our country out of the economic doldrums in which it is stuck. Nor will it win the support of foreign allies or respect of foreign adversaries. President Obama entered the Oval Office facing a number of major tests—tests he must pass for the good of our country. Credibility, trustworthy character, a realistic understanding of the nature of man, a sound knowledge of American history as well as world history, and adherence to Godly principles would enable President Obama to pass the tests. Unfortunately for America, President Obama is failing these tests.